P9-DMA-993

STONEHAM PUBLIC LIBRARY
431 MAIN STREET
STONEHAM, MA 02180

PARTY KNITS

DATE DUE

JUL 2 5 2014

GAYLORD   #3523PI   Printed in USA

PARTY KNITS

MELODY GRIFFITHS & LESLEY STANFIELD

CREATIVE
HOMEOWNER®

First published in North America in 2007 by

CRE▲TIVE
HOMEOWNER®

Upper Saddle River, NJ
Creative Homeowner® is a registered trademark of
Federal Marketing Corporation

Copyright © 2007 text and designs
Melody Griffiths and Lesley Stanfield
Copyright © 2007 photographs
New Holland Publishers (UK) Ltd
Copyright © 2007 New Holland Publishers (UK) Ltd

All rights reserved. No part of this publication may
be reproduced, stored in a retrieval system, or transmitted
in any form or by any means, electronic, mechanical,
photocopying, recording, or otherwise, without the prior
written permission of the publishers and copyright holders.
Current printing (last digit): 10 9 8 7 6 5 4 3 2 1
Library of Congress card number: 2006929063
ISBN-10: 1-58011-329-X
ISBN-13: 978-1-58011-329-8

Senior editor: Clare Hubbard
Photographer: Sian Irvine
Designer: Isobel Gillan
Production: Hazel Kirkman
Editorial direction: Rosemary Wilkinson

Reproduction by Pica Digital PTE Ltd, Singapore
Printed and bound by Times Offset, Malaysia

CREATIVE HOMEOWNER
A division of Federal Marketing Corp.
24 Park Way
Upper Saddle River, NJ 07458
www.creativehomeowner.com

Contents

Introduction

This is a collection of simple, inspired ideas to set your imagination racing. Knitwear can be curvy, cozy, decorated, textured, classic, clinging, see-through, or sophisticated. It can flatter your best features, or shift the focus away from areas you want to hide. It can express your individuality whether you want to dress up or dress down. Best of all, hand knitting gives you the opportunity to create unique, luxurious clothes.

Here you'll find everything you need for that special occasion. From simple accessories to stunning sweaters and jackets, there are 25 up-to-the-minute stylish fashion items. All can be made using the basic knitting skills outlined in the clear and concise Getting Started section (see pages 10–21), which includes extra explanation to help with any less familiar techniques.

There are three style sections to explore. All include designs for extra special evenings and for those daytime occasions when you want something a little dressier —from sexy shapes and daring body-conscious garments to fashion knits in fancy yarns; from subtle beaded decoration to all-over sequins—there's something for every type of party.

Choose the style that enhances your look and make it in the color that suits you. Mix your knits with basic black or fabulous fabrics; pile on the jewelry or leave them plain. And when you've invested the time and care in making these knits you'll find that they are fashion classics that will last many years, precious possessions that you'll wear over and over again.

Equipment

All you need to create beautiful hand knits is some yarn, knitting needles, simple sewing equipment, and patience!

YARNS

The designs in this book feature classic and fashion yarns. Enjoy the feel of luxury mixes such as cashmere, alpaca, and silk; choose shimmering metallic, smooth cotton, or man-made fibers with fabulous furry textures. Each design has been created with the particular qualities of the chosen yarn in mind. Ideally, you should always use the yarn specified, although the choice of color is up to you! But fashion yarns and colors change with the seasons, so if you do need to find a substitute yarn, check that the fiber content, yarn type, texture, and number of yards (meters) in a ball match the original as closely as possible.

These are the yarns used in this book:
- **Debbie Bliss Alpaca Silk DK** 80% baby alpaca, 20% silk. 115 yd (105 m) per 50 g (1.76 oz) ball.
- **Debbie Bliss Cathay:** 50% cotton, 35% micro-fiber, 15% silk. 110 yd (100 m) per 50 g (1.76 oz) ball.
- **Debbie Bliss Pure Silk:** 100% silk. 140 yd (125 m) per 50 g (1.76 oz) hank.
- **Rowan Denim:** 100% cotton. 102 yd (93 m) per 50 g (1.76 oz) ball.
- **Crystal Palace Shag:** 45% wool, 45% acrylic, 10% nylon, 57 yd (52 m) per 50 g (1.76 oz) ball.

- **Rowan Lurex Shimmer:** 80% viscose, 20% polyester. 105 yd (95 m) per 25 g (0.88 oz) ball.
- **Rowan Kid Silk Haze:** 70% super kid mohair, 30% silk. 230 yd (210 m) per 25 g (0.88 oz) ball.
- **RYC Cashsoft DK:** 57% extra fine merino, 33% microfiber, 10% cashmere. 145 yd (130 m) per 50 g (1.76 oz) ball.
- **RYC Soft Lux:** 64% extra fine merino wool, 10% angora, 24% nylon, 2% metallic fiber. 140 yd (125 m) per 50 g (1.76 oz) ball.
- **Crystal Palace Splash:** 100% polyester. 94 yd (85 m) per 50 g (1.76 oz) ball.
- **Classic Elite Provence:** 100% cotton. 205 yd (338 m) per 100 g (3.53 oz) ball.
- **Lana Grossa Meilenweit 100:** 80% wool, 20% polyamid. 459 yd (420 m) per 100 g (3.53 oz) ball.
- **Lion Brand Microspun:** 100% acrylic. 168 yd (154 m) per 70 g (2.47 oz) ball.
- **Karabella Piuma Gold:** 60% kid mohair, 20% metallic, 20% polyester.. 108 yd (99 m) per 50 g (1.76 oz) ball.

NEEDLES

A pair of straight needles is the type most often used, but for some of the projects you will also need a circular needle, a set of double pointed needles, or a cable needle. Experiment with different lengths of straight needles to find the type that are most comfortable for you. Remember that circular needles can be used for flat knitting as well as for working in the round.

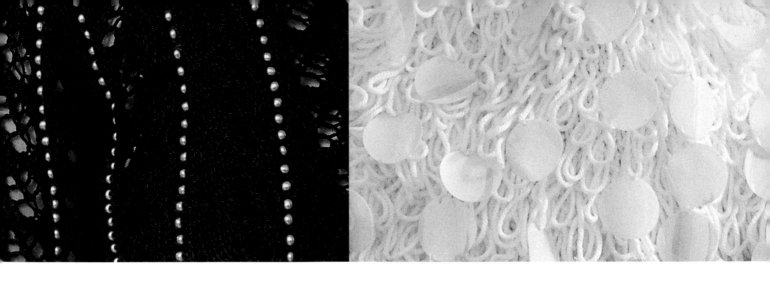

The needle size given in the instructions is the size that the knitter used to get the gauge given when the sample garment was made. This needle size should be treated only as a guide; the size you need to use is the size that gives you the correct gauge. If you're going out to buy needles, it makes sense to get one or two sizes above and below the recommended size. This way you'll soon build up a collection.

ACCESSORIES

You'll need a tape measure to check your gauge and garment measurements, and scissors to cut the yarn. A stitch holder can be useful, but you can always improvise with a circular needle or a length of yarn. Markers help keep track of the rows when shaping, or the stitches when working pattern repeats. Use the plastic hook-on type, safety pins, or loops of smooth contrast yarn. A blunt-pointed wool needle is essential for sewing up; a sharp pointed needle will split the stitches. Large-headed pins set at right-angles to the seam keep the pieces in place when sewing them up, especially when fitting a sleeve head into the armhole. A slim tapestry needle will slip through the holes more easily when sewing on buttons.

BEADS AND SEQUINS

From scattered decoration to all-over coverage, even the simplest knits get the glamor treatment with added beads and sequins. Some of these designs have beads or sequins knitted in; others have the decoration sewn on after the knitting is finished. You can choose from a variety of different types—glass, metallic, or plastic—and shapes of beads. Most of the round beads used in this book are rocaille or embroidery beads, often described as size 5 or 5/0. These can be sewn on or knitted in. Where you need a larger quantity of beads for knitting in, you'll find that buying beads in packs of 300 g (10.58 oz) or 500 g (17.63 oz) is cheaper than buying lots of small tubes, even if some beads are left over. Finer seed beads and bugle beads are only suitable for sewing on. Buying small packs makes sense because you will have greater choice. You could also recycle broken necklaces or use antique beads to give a vintage effect.

When buying beads or sequins, take a ball of the yarn along with you to be sure that they match or contrast with the color of the yarn and that, if necessary, the hole in the beads is big enough to thread them onto the yarn. Sequins are made in many different shapes and sizes: round flat, round cupped, square, or oval. Any type of sequin can be sewn on, and it can often be effective to use several related shades in a design. The round, flat sequins for knitting in are usually sold in strands of 1,000. Check when you buy to ensure that they are on a thread, not loose in a pack, because this will make it a lot easier to thread them onto the yarn. If you are matching sequins and yarn, always choose a yarn color that is darker than the sequins—a lighter shade will dominate the sequin color.

Getting Started

FOLLOWING THE INSTRUCTIONS

Before you start to knit, read through the instructions to be sure that you understand the abbreviations and you can cope with all the techniques needed.

Abbreviations are used for many of the repetitive words that occur in the instructions. See the box, right, for the most frequently used abbreviations; any additional abbreviations are given with the instructions. Some abbreviations look complex but make sense once you realize that they explain a series of actions, such as skp for slip one stitch knitwise, knit one stitch, pass the slipped stitch over.

Brackets are used to show how many times a series of stitches should be worked or to clarify working a group of stitches. Brackets are also placed around stitch counts. Asterisks indicate where to repeat instructions from or which part of the instructions to work again.

Check that you know which measurements you are working to. The amount of movement room varies according to the design, so if you are not sure which size to make, check the actual measurements given against an existing garment that fits you well.

Where instructions for different sizes are given, the smallest size is given first, followed by the other sizes in parentheses, separated by colons. If there is only one figure, it refers to all of the sizes.

ABBREVIATIONS

beg – beginning	rem – remaining
cont – continu(e)(ing)	rep – repeat
dec – decreas(e)(ing)	RS – right side
foll – following	sl – slip
inc – increas(e)(ing)	skp – slip one knitwise,
inc 1 – knit into front	knit one, pass slipped
and back of stitch	stitch over
k – knit	st(s) – stitch(es)
m1 – make a stitch by	St st – stockinette stitch
lifting strand between	tbl – through back of
stitches and knitting	loop(s)
into the back of it	tog – together
p – purl	WS – wrong side
patt – pattern	yo – yarn over needle to
	make a stitch

CHECKING YOUR GAUGE

This is the job that you may want to avoid. But you really must make sure that your gauge matches the gauge given or your garment will not be the correct size. Start with the needle size given and knit a swatch in the stitch pattern given for the item. The instructions under gauge tell you how many stitches and how many rows make a 4 in. (10 cm) square, but cast on slightly more stitches and work a few more rows than given because the stitches at the edge will distort. Count and mark the correct number of stitches and rows from the center of the swatch. If your marked stitches and rows measure less than they should, your knitting is too tight and the garment will be too small, so try again using larger needles. If they measure more, your knitting is too loose and the garment will be too big. Try again using smaller needles. It can be difficult to see the stitches in some textured yarns so try holding the swatch up to the light to count and mark the stitches and rows, then lay it flat to measure.

BASIC TECHNIQUES

Here's a reminder of the essential knitting techniques:

MAKING A SLIP KNOT

A slip knot counts as the first stitch.

Leaving an end that's long enough to cast on the required number of stitches, make a loop in the yarn. Insert the tip of the right needle and pull a loop through. Gently pull on the yarn to tighten the knot and to close the loop on the needle.

CASTING ON

Knitting into a loop around the thumb to make a stitch on the needle is the easiest and most versatile method of casting on.

After making a slip knot, hold the needle and the yarn from the ball in the right or left hand. Using the long end, make a loop around the left thumb and insert the right needle tip. Bring the yarn up between the thumb and needle and take it around the needle.

Draw the yarn through to make a stitch on the needle, release the loop from the left thumb, and tighten the long end ready to make the next stitch.

MAKING A KNIT STITCH—WITH YARN IN RIGHT HAND

Hold the needle with the cast-on stitches in the left hand and the empty needle in the right hand. The yarn from the ball is at the back and is held in the right hand.

Bring the right needle forward and, taking it under the left needle, insert it from left to right into the front of the first stitch. Take the yarn up and around the right needle.

With the tip of the right needle, draw a loop of yarn forward through the stitch on the left needle. Then drop stitch off the left needle, and gauge the yarn to make a stitch on the right needle. Work into each stitch on the left needle in turn to complete a knit row.

MAKING A PURL STITCH—WITH YARN IN RIGHT HAND

Hold the needles in the same way as for making a knit stitch, but bring the yarn from the ball to the front.

Taking the right needle under the left, insert it from right to left into the front of the first stitch, taking the yarn over and around the right needle.

Dip the tip of the right needle away from you to draw a loop of yarn through the stitch on the left needle, then drop the stitch off the left needle and gauge the yarn to make a stitch on the right needle. Work into each stitch on the left needle in turn to complete a purl row.

MAKING A KNIT STITCH
WITH THE YARN IN LEFT HAND

Hold the needle with the cast-on stitches in the left hand and the empty needle in the right hand. The yarn from the ball is at the back and is held in the left hand, taut over the first finger.

Bring the right needle forward and, taking it under the left needle, insert it from left to right into the front of the first stitch. Then hook the right needle over and under the yarn.

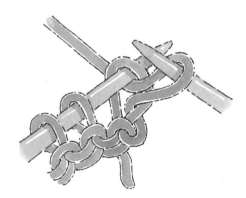

With the tip of the right needle, draw a loop of yarn forward and through the stitch on the left needle. Then drop the stitch off the left needle, and gauge the yarn to make a stitch on the right needle. Work into each stitch in turn to complete a knit row.

MAKING A PURL STITCH
WITH THE YARN IN LEFT HAND

Hold the needles in the same way as for a knit stitch, but bring the yarn from the ball to the front and hold it in the left hand, taut over the first finger.

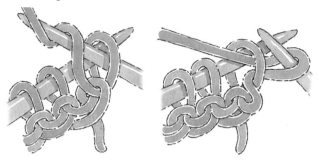

Taking the right needle under the left, insert it from right to left into the first stitch, then hook the right needle over and under the yarn. Dip the tip of the right needle downwards and away from you to draw a loop of yarn through the stitch on the left needle, then drop the stitch off the left needle and gauge the yarn to make a stitch on the right needle. Work into each stitch on the left needle in turn to complete a purl row.

BINDING OFF

Lifting one stitch over the next secures the stitches and makes a neat edge. Working every stitch as a knit stitch will give a chain edge; binding off in purl will give a bumpy edge.

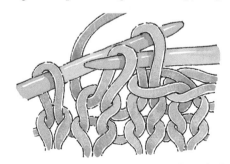

Knit two stitches. Use the point of the left needle to lift the first stitch over the second and off the needle. Knit the next stitch so there are two stitches on the right needle. Lift one stitch over and off the right needle. Continue until one stitch is left on the right needle. Break the yarn, draw the end through, and pull tight.

SPECIAL TECHNIQUES

This section leads you through a variety of ways to manipulate stitches to create everything from the subtlest shaping to delicate lace stitches or rich surface textures.

INCREASING

Simple increases make one stitch. The first method makes a little bar at the base of the new stitch, the second is almost invisible, and the third makes a decorative hole. More complex increases make two or more stitches integrated with the shaping or patterning.

Single increase: inc 1

Knitting into the front and back of a stitch makes two stitches from one.

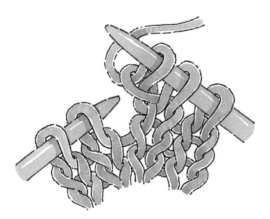

Knit a stitch, but do not allow the stitch to drop off the left needle. Take the right needle tip behind the left to knit into the back of the same stitch, then drop the stitch off the left needle.

Single increase: m1

Working into the strand lying between stitches is a neat way to increase one stitch. Make sure that the strand crosses over at the base of the new stitch or you'll make a hole in the work.

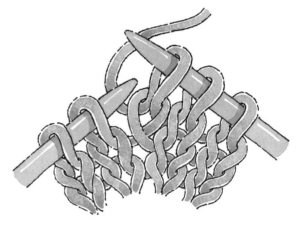

Bring the left needle forward, and, inserting the tip from the front to back of the work, lift the strand from between the needles. Take the right needle behind to knit into the back of the strand. If you want the strand to cross over in the opposite direction, place the strand on the left needle in the opposite direction and work into the front of it. This type of increase can also be worked as a purl stitch; lift the strand in the same way, then purl into the back of it.

Single increase: yo

Taking the yarn around the needle makes a stitch with a decorative hole at the base. Larger holes can be made by working more yarn-overs.

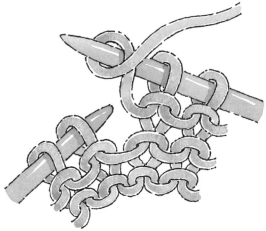

Between a purl and a purl, take the yarn over the needle and to the front again ready to purl the next stitch.

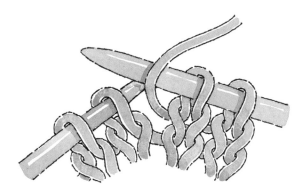

Between two knit stitches, bring the yarn between the needles to the front of the work and over the needle ready to knit the next stitch.

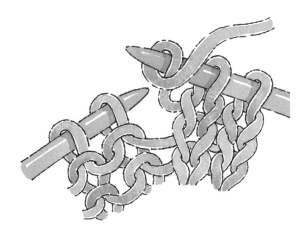

Between a knit and a purl stitch, bring the yarn to the front, over the needle, and to the front again ready to purl the next stitch.

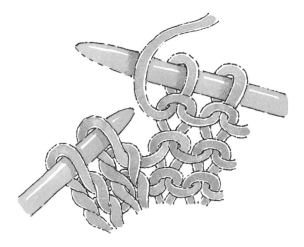

Between a purl and a knit stitch, the yarn is already at the front of the work; take it over the needle ready to knit the next stitch. Work this yarn over loosely or it will appear to be smaller than the other types of yarn over.

Double increase: d inc

This method makes 3 stitches from one stitch, almost invisibly.

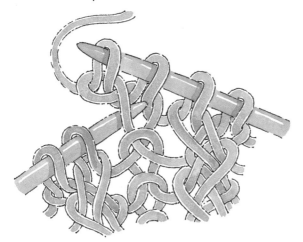

Knit in to the back and front of the stitch, then insert the left needle tip behind the vertical strand that runs downward from between the two stitches just made and knit in to the back of this strand.

DECREASING

Simple decreases take two stitches together to make one stitch. The first two methods are mirror images usually worked in pairs to give a fully fashioned effect. More complex two-stitch decreases can be used for both shaping and patterning.

Single decrease: k2tog

Knitting two stitches together is the easiest way to decrease one stitch. The second stitch lies on top and the decrease slants to the right.

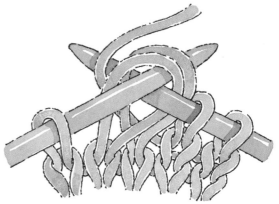

Insert the right needle through the fronts of the next two stitches on the left needle, then knit the stitch in the usual way, slipping both stitches off the left needle together.

Single decrease: skp

Slip one stitch knitwise, knit one stitch, pass the slipped stitch over to make the mirror image of k2tog. The first stitch lies on top and the decrease slants to the left.

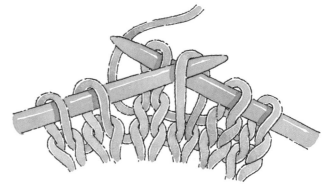

Slip the first stitch, knit the next stitch, use the tip of the left needle to lift the slipped stitch over and off the right needle.

Double decrease: sk2p

Slip one, knit two together, pass the slipped stitch over is the easiest way to take three stitches together. The first stitch lies on top, the third stitch is next, and the second stitch is at the back; the decrease slants to the left.

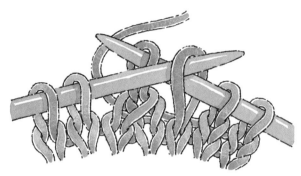

Slip the first stitch, knit the next two stitches together, then use the tip of the left needle to lift the slipped stitch over and off the right needle.

Double decrease: s2kpo

Slip two stitches, knit one, pass the slipped stitches over is another way to take three stitches together. The center stitch lies on top.

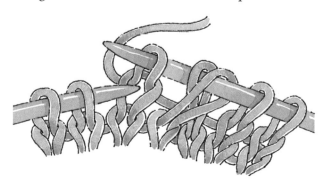

Insert the right needle through the fronts of the first two stitches on the left needle as if to knit two together, then slip these stitches onto the right needle, knit the next stitch, use the tip of the left needle to lift the two slipped stitches over and off the right needle.

CABLES

Cable stitch patterns are made by using a short double-pointed needle to change the place of two or more stitches in a row. Cables can be worked with knit stitches only or with a combination of knit and purl stitches.

Cable back: c4b

This cable slants to the right.

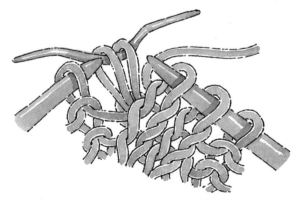

Slip the next two stitches onto a cable needle, hold the cable needle at the back of the work, knit the next two stitches on the left needle, then knit the two stitches from the cable needle and continue the row.

Cable front: c4f

This cable slants to the left.

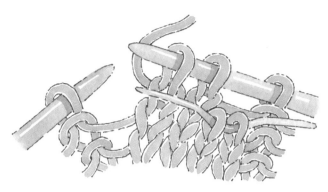

Slip the next two stitches onto a cable needle, hold the cable needle at the front of the work, knit the next two stitches on the left needle, then knit the two stitches from the cable needle and continue the row.

Twists

Twist stitch patterns are made by knitting or purling the stitches in a different order.

Knit twist: t2k

This method twists two stitches knitwise on right side rows.

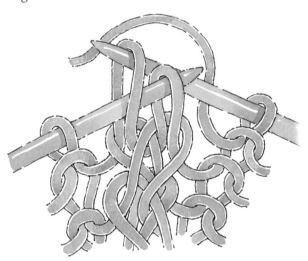

Take the needle behind the first stitch on the lefthand needle, and knit in to the back of the second stitch; bring the needle forward and knit in to the front of the first stitch; and slip both stitches off the left needle together.

Purl twist: t2p

This twists two stitches purlwise on wrong side rows.

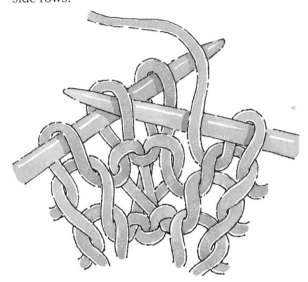

Take the needle in front of the first stitch on the lefthand needle to purl the second stitch, then purl the first stitch and slip both stitches off the left needle together.

Loop stitch

This method of making a single loop is very stable; it won't stretch or slip back and open up the fabric.

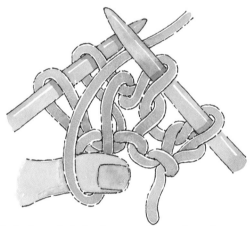

Knit the stitch in the usual way, but do not allow it to drop off the left needle; bring the yarn to the front between the needles, then take it under then over the left thumb and back between the needles; knit the stitch on the left needle again, and slip it off in the usual way; then lift the previous stitch on the right needle over it.

DECORATIVE EFFECTS

Beads and sequins can be knitted in or sewn on. For all-over beads and sequins, thread them onto the yarn before starting to knit. If the yarn is fine you may be able to thread directly onto the yarn with a fine needle; if not, use the following method. When sewing on beads and sequins, match the thread as closely as possible and use a small, sharp-pointed needle.

THREADING BEADS OR SEQUINS

Using an intermediary loop of thread makes it easier to slip the beads or sequins onto the yarn.

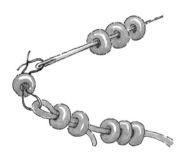

Thread a fine needle with a short length of strong sewing thread, knot the ends together, and slide the knot to the side. Pass the end of the yarn through the loop of thread. Pick up the beads or groups of sequins onto the needle, slide them over the loop of thread, and down onto the yarn.

KNITTING IN BEADS

The simplest way of knitting with beads is to work them between stitches.

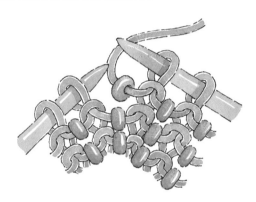

Work until ready to place a bead, bring a bead up close to the knitting, then work the next stitch so the bead hangs between the stitches. This can be done on knit or purl rows, but the beads show up more between purl stitches.

SEWING ON BEADS

Using the backstitch anchors beads firmly.

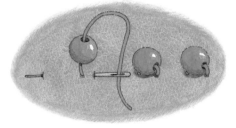

Bring the needle out where the bead is to be positioned, insert the needle through the bead, and, holding the bead close to the work, insert the needle just behind the bead, ready to be brought out where the next bead is required.

KNITTING IN SEQUINS

Sequin knitting is basically just stockinette stitch. Bringing a sequin through to the right side of the work as you knit a stitch makes the sequin lie flat on the front of the knitting. Working the stitch through the back of the loop is not necessary for all yarns, but it will help stop the sequin from slipping through to the wrong side when working with a smooth yarn.

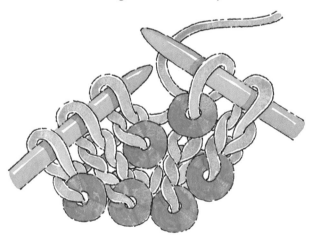

Work until you are ready to place a sequin, insert the left needle into the back of the next stitch, bring a sequin up close to the work, and slip the sequin through to the right side as you knit the stitch.

SEWING ON SEQUINS

Sequins can be sewn on with the backstitch in the same way as beads, but holding the sequin in place with a seed bead is more decorative and hides the sewing yarn and the hole in the sequin.

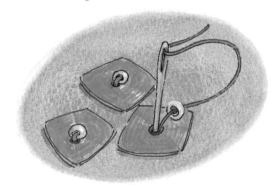

Place the sequin. Bring the needle up through the hole in the center of the sequin, then slide a bead onto the needle and down the thread. Take the needle around the bead and back down into the hole. Pull the thread taut to bring the bead close to the sequin, and secure it on the wrong side with a few backstitches before moving onto the next sequin.

FINISHING

Each set of instructions explains the best way to put the knitted sesctions together, but here are some general points about making up knits.

Ironing

Blocking the pieces by pinning them out to shape and steam ironing on the wrong side before making up gives a professional finish, especially for garments in natural fibers. Iron the seams as you construct the garment. Always check the yarn care instructions on the ball band, because yarns in manmade fibers often cannot be ironed—in which case they can be blocked to size, sprayed lightly with water, and allowed to dry to set the shapes before sewing them up. Beaded knits can be ironed on the wrong side, using a press cloth to protect the surface. But garments covered in sequins should never be ironed.

Sewing seams

The best way to sew seams in knitting is to work with the right side facing you so you can match stitches or row-ends for an almost invisible join. Using the tail of yarn left over from casting on or binding off makes a neat start. To join a new length of yarn, simply run the needle through a few edge stitches before bringing the needle up to continue stitching. When the sewing is complete, darn in the ends from joining new balls of yarn along the seams, not along the rows.

Mattress stitch

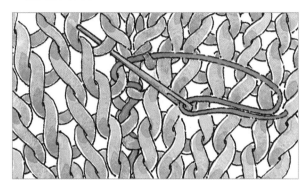

Use this to join the side and the sleeve seams. Working from side to side alternately, insert the needle under the strand between the stitches, one stitch in from the edge. Every two or three stitches, pull the yarn taut to bring the edges together.

GARMENT CARE

Store knits folded flat. To deter moths, products with essential oils and Neem can be placed in protective bags and stored with the knits. Make sure that your knits are scrupulously clean before putting them away.

Before washing garments, always remember to turn them inside out. Garments without decoration can be washed according to the yarn manufacturer's instructions. Decorated garments should be washed by hand; check first that any beads are colorfast. Dry garments flat whenever possible.

Some types of beads should not be washed; check the appropriate care when you buy them.

JEWEL COLORS

Stand out from the crowd in striking shades of ruby red, sapphire blue, hot pink, lime green, magenta, and purple, or go for the subtle approach with opal green and rose-quartz pink. Choose a cropped camisole or a cover-up cardigan coat in the softest pastel shades; slip into sexy shapes in classic yarns with an off-the-shoulder top and a dramatic V-back slimline sweater; or revel in vibrant tones and textures with a skimpy shrug in fine mohair, a ruffled-edge bolero, a fur coat, and a velvet-effect jacket. Finally, accent your look with a bright beaded bag or a fun flower corsage.

The yarn is so chunky that you need very few stitches to create this fabulous furry coat. It's just the right length to wear over pants or with more formal evening clothes.

Fun Fur Coat

EASY

MEASUREMENTS

To fit bust

34–36	38–40	42–44	46–48	in.
86–91	97–102	107–112	117–122	cm

Actual bust

39$^{1}/_{2}$	43$^{1}/_{2}$	47$^{1}/_{4}$	51$^{1}/_{4}$	in.
100	110	120	130	cm

Actual length

39	40	41	41$^{3}/_{4}$	in.
99.5	102	104	106.5	cm

Actual sleeve length

20 in

51 cm

In the instructions, figures are given for the smallest size first; larger sizes follow in brackets. Where only one set of figures is given, this applies to all sizes.

MATERIALS

- 10 (24:26:28) × 50 g (1.76 oz) balls of Crystal Palace Shag in Canyon, 7207
- Pair of US 15 (10 mm) needles
- Kilt pin or brooch

GAUGE

8 sts and 9 rows to 4 in. (10 cm) over St st on US 15 (10 mm) needles. Change needle size if necessary to obtain this gauge.

ABBREVIATIONS

[ ]—work instructions in square brackets as directed. *See page 10.*

NOTES

- Actual bust measurement is calculated with seam stitches taken off and fronts wrapped over.
- When knitted, Shag is so textured that it is quite hard to see the stitches and rows. To check your gauge, cast on 10 sts, work in St st 11 rows, and bind off. Place markers one stitch in from each edge and one row in from cast-on and bind-off edges, measure each way. If you get less than 4 in. (10 cm) try again using larger needles; if you get more than 4 in. (10 cm), try again using smaller needles.
- Shapings are given on knit rows because this is easier to work, but make up the coat with the reverse side of stockinette stitch as the right side to show the furry texture.

Take the yarn end from the center of the ball; it will stop the ball from rolling around and picking up dirt and scraps as you knit.

Place markers at each end of the shaping rows on the back and sleeves and at the side edges on the fronts to help keep track of the rows between increases or decreases.

BACK

Cast on 56 (60:64:68) sts.

Beg k row, work in St st until back measures 4¹/₄ in. (11 cm), ending with a p row.

1st dec row: (WS) K1, k2tog, k15 (16:17:18), k2tog, k16 (18:20:22), skp, k15 (16:17:18), skp, k1. [52 (56:60:64) sts.]

Work in St st for 9 rows.

2nd dec row: (WS) K1, k2tog, k13 (14:15:16), k2tog, k16 (18:20:22), skp, k13 (14:15:16), skp, k1. [48 (52:56:60) sts.]

Work in St st for 9 rows.

3rd dec row: (WS) K1, k2tog, k11 (12:13:14), k2tog, k16 (18:20:22), skp, k11 (12:13:14), skp, k1. [44 (48:52:56) sts.]

Work in St st for 7 rows.

4th dec row: (WS) K1, k2tog, k9 (10:11:12), k2tog, k16 (18:20:22), skp, k9 (10:11:12), skp, k1. [40 (44:48:52) sts.]

Work in St st for 5 rows.

5th dec row: (WS) K1, k2tog, k7 (8:9:10), k2tog, k16 (18:20:22), skp, k7 (8:9:10), skp, k1. [36 (40:44:48) sts.]

Work in St st for 7 rows.

Inc row: (WS) Inc 1, k to last 2 sts, inc 1, k1.

Cont in St st, inc in this way at each end of every 4th row 2 times. [42 (46:50:54) sts.]

Work in St st for 5 rows.

Shape armholes

Bind off 2 sts at beg of next 2 rows.

Dec row: (WS) K1, k2tog, k to last 3 sts, skp, k1.

Cont in St st, dec in this way at each end of next 2 (3:4:5) WS rows. [32 (34:36:38) sts.]

Work in St st for 17 rows. Bind off.

RIGHT FRONT

Cast on 31 (33:35:37) sts.

Beg k row, work in St st until front measures 4¹/₄ in. (11 cm), ending with a p row.

1st dec row: (WS) K1, k2tog, k15 (16:17:18), k2tog, k11 (12:13:14). [29 (31:33:35) sts.]

Work in St st for 9 rows.

2nd dec row: (WS) K1, k2tog, k13 (14:15:16), k2tog, k11 (12:13:14). [27 (29:31:33) sts.]

Work in St st for 9 rows.

3rd dec row: (WS) K1, k2tog, k11 (12:13:14), k2tog, k11 (12:13:14). [25 (27:29:31) sts.]

Work in St st for 7 rows.

4th dec row: (WS) K1, k2tog, k9 (10:11:12), k2tog, k11 (12:13:14). [23 (25:27:29) sts.]

Work in St st for 5 rows.

5th dec row: (WS) K1, k2tog, k7 (8:9:10), k2tog, k11 (12:13:14). [21 (23:25:27) sts.]

Work in St st 7 rows.

Inc row: (RS) Inc 1, k to end.

Cont in St sst, inc in this way at beg of every 4th row 2 times. [24 (26:28:30) sts.]

Work in St st for 5 rows.

Shape armhole

Bind off 2 sts at beg of next row. P 1 row.

Dec row: (WS) K1, k2tog, k to end.

Cont in St st, dec in this way at beg of next 2 (3:4:5) RS rows. [19 (20:21:22) sts.]

Work in St st for 5 rows.

Join seams with the right sides facing, using the mattress stitch. Match and remove the markers as you sew up the sections.

If your gauge is just a little bit off, try holding the yarn more tightly or more loosely rather than changing needle size.

If you don't want to pin the front sections, buy matching ribbon and make ties.

Shape collar

Inc row: (RS) K to last 2 sts, inc 1, k1.
Cont in St st, inc in this way at end of next 3 WS rows. [23 (24:25:26) sts.] P 1 row.

Shape neck

1st row: (WS) K11 (12:13:14), bind off 12.
2nd row: (RS) Join yarn, p2tog, p to end.
3rd row: K to last 2 sts, skp.
4th row: P2tog, p to end. [8 (9:10:11) sts.] Bind off.

LEFT FRONT

Cast on 31 (33:35:37) sts.
Beg k row, St st until front measures 4¼ in. (11 cm), ending with a p row.
1st dec row: (WS) K11 (12:13:14), skp, k15 (16:17:18), skp, k1. [29 (31:33:35) sts.] Work in St st for 9 rows.
2nd dec row: (WS) K11 (12:13:14), skp, k13 (14:15:16), skp, k1. [27 (29:31:33) sts.] Work in St st for 9 rows.
3rd dec row: (WS) K11 (12:13:14), skp, k11 (12:13:14), skp, k1. [25 (27:29:31) sts.] Work in St st for 7 rows.
4th dec row: (WS) K11 (12:13:14), skp, k9 (10:11:12), skp, k1. [23 (25:27:29) sts.] Work in St st for 5 rows.
5th dec row: (WS) K11 (12:13:14), skp, k7 (8:9:10), skp, k1. [21 (23:25:27) sts.] Work in St st for 7 rows.
Inc row: (WS) K to last 2 sts, inc 1, k1. Cont in St st, inc in this way at end of every 4th row 2 times. [24 (26:28:30) sts.] Work in St st for 6 rows.

Shape armhole

Bind off 2 sts at beg of next row.
Dec row: (WS) K to last 3 sts, skp, k1.
Cont in St st, dec in this way at end of next 2 (3:4:5) WS rows. [19 (20:21:22) sts.] Work in St st for 5 rows.

Shape collar

Inc row: (WS) Inc 1, k to end.
Cont in St st, inc in this way at beg of next 3 WS rows. [23 (24:25:26) sts.] P 1 row.

Shape neck

1st row: (WS) Bind off 12 sts, k to end. [11 (12:13:14) sts.]
2nd row: P to last 2 sts, p2tog.
3rd row: K2tog, k to end.
4th row: P to last 2 sts, p2tog. [8 (9:10:11) sts.] Bind off.

SLEEVES

Cast on 20 (22:24:26) sts. Beg k row, work in St st until sleeve measures 5 in. (13 cm), ending with a p row.
Inc row: (WS) Inc 1, k to last 2 sts, inc 1, k1.
Cont in St st, inc in this way at each end of every 6th row 4 times. [30 (32:34:36) sts.] Work in St st until sleeve measures 20 in. (51 cm), ending with a p row.

Shape top

Bind off 2 sts at beg of next 2 rows.

Dec row: (WS) K1, k2tog, k to last 3 sts, skp, k1.
Cont in St st, dec in this way at each end of next 2 (3:4:5) WS rows. [20 sts.] P 1 row.

Next row: (WS) Slipping first st, bind off 2 sts, k to last 2 sts, skp. [17 sts.]

Next row: Slipping first st, bind off 2 sts, p to last 2 sts, p2tog. [14 sts.]
Work last 2 rows again. [8 sts.] Bind off.

COLLAR

Matching sts, join shoulders. With WS facing, beg at 6th st from front edge of left front collar, k 13 sts up left front neck, 16 sts across back neck, and 13 sts down right front neck, ending at 6th st from front edge. [42 sts.] Beg p row, work in St st for 8 rows. Bind off.

TO MAKE UP

Set in sleeves. Join side and sleeve seams, reversing seam for turn-back cuff if wished.

Choose yarns in vibrant reds or soft pinks to make this light-hearted woolly flower decoration.

Rose Corsage

 EASY

MEASUREMENTS
The flower is about 2³/₄ in. (7 cm) across.

MATERIALS
- Oddments of DK yarn in pink and green
- Pair of US 5 (3³/₄ mm) knitting needles
- Small safety pin

ABBREVIATIONS
See page 10.

GAUGE
21 sts and 36 rows to 4 in. (10 cm) over g-st on US 5 (3³/₄ mm) needles.

CENTER PETALS (make 3)
With deep pink, cast on 3 sts.
1st row: Inc 1 twice, k1. [5 sts.]
2nd row: K.
3rd row: Inc 1, k2, inc 1, k1. [7 sts.]
4th row: K.
5th row: Inc 1, k4, inc 1, k1. [9 sts.]
6th row: K.
7th row: K1, [k2tog] 4 times. [5 sts.]
8th row: K.
9th row: K1, [k2tog] twice. [3 sts.]
10th row: K.
Break yarn and leave sts on a spare needle.
Leave second and third petals on same needle.

OUTER PETALS (make 5)
With paler pink, cast on 5 sts.
1st row: Inc 1 4 times, k1. [9 sts.]
2nd row: K.
3rd row: Inc 1, k6, inc 1, k1. [11 sts.]
4th–8th rows: K.
9th row: K1, [k2tog] 5 times. [6 sts.]
10th row: K.
11th row: K1, [k2tog] twice, k1. [4 sts.]
12th row: K.
Break yarn and leave sts on a spare needle. Leave second, third, fourth, and fifth petals on same needle.

BASE
Darn in cast-on ends of yarn on each petal. With deep pink, k sts of each petal in turn, starting with 5 outer petals and ending with 3 center petals. [29 sts.]
K 2 rows.
Bind off, working k2tog to last st, k 1. Break yarn, leaving an end long enough to sew with. Darn in remaining petal ends.
Coil into a ring, alternating petals as far as possible, then use long end to secure by stitching base.
To hold petals in half-open position, use paler pink to stitch outer petals to each other at a point about halfway up the petal.

LEAVES (make 3)

With green, cast on 10 sts.

1st row: Inc 1, k7, k2tog.

2nd row: K.

Repeat these 2 rows 4 times more, then work 1st row again.

Bind off knitwise.

Make second piece the same, then stitch both pieces together around the edges.

TO MAKE UP

Attach leaves to rose. Stitch safety pin to underside.

Making petals and leaves requires some careful darning in of ends, but the rose is really very easy to knit.

Soft alpaca-silk-mix yarn makes a drapey fabric with a subtle sheen, perfect for this easy-to-wear top.

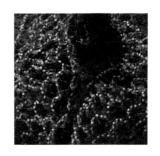

Ruffle-Edge Bolero

MEASUREMENTS

To fit bust

32	34	36	38	40	42	in.
81	86	91	97	102	107	cm

Actual bust

33	35$^1/_2$	37$^1/_2$	39$^3/_4$	41$^3/_4$	44	in.
84	90	95	101	106	112	cm

Actual length

24	24$^1/_4$	24$^3/_4$	25$^1/_4$	25$^1/_2$	26	in.
61	61.5	63	64	65	66.5	cm

In the instructions, figures are given for the smallest size first; larger sizes follow in brackets. Where only one figure is given, this applies to all sizes.

MATERIALS

- 7 (8:8:9:10:11) × 50 g (1.76 oz) balls of Debbie Bliss Alpaca Silk DK in magenta, 007
- Pair of US 6 (4 mm) needles
- US 6 (4 mm) circular needles, 39$^1/_2$ in. (100 cm) and 15$^3/_4$ in. (40 cm) long
- 2$^1/_4$ yd (2 m) stretch lace for tie

GAUGE

20 sts and 28 rows to 4 in. (10 cm) over lace patt, 22 sts and 28 rows to 4 in. (10 cm) over St st, both on US 6 (4 mm) needles. Change needle size if necessary to obtain these gauges.

ABBREVIATIONS

m1k—lift strand between sts and k into back of it; **m1p**—lift strand between sts and p into back of it; **sk2p**—slip one knitwise, k2tog, pass slipped st over; [ ]—work instructions in brackets as directed. _See also page 10._

BACK

Cast on 82 (86:92:98:104:110) sts.
1st row: (RS) K4 (6:9:12:15:18), [yo, p2tog, k7] 8 times, yo, p2tog, k4 (6:9:12:15:18).
2nd, 4th, and 6th rows: P4 (6:9:12:15:18), [yo, p2tog, p7] 8 times, yo, p2tog, p4 (6:9:12:15:18).
3rd row: K4 (6:9:12:15:18), [yo, p2tog, k3, yo, k2tog, k2] 8 times, yo, p2tog, k4 (6:9:12:15:18).
5th row: K4 (6:9:12:15:18), * yo, p2tog, k2, [yo, k2tog] twice, k1, rep from * 7 more times, yo, p2tog, k4 (6:9:12:15:18).
These 6 rows form lace patt with St st at each side. Patt 6 more rows.
Dec row: (RS) K2, k2tog, patt to last 4 sts, skp, k2.
1st size only: Cont in patt, work 29 rows.
All other sizes: Cont in patt, dec in this way at each end of every 10th row 2 times. Patt 9 rows.
All sizes: [80 (80:86:92:98:104) sts.]
Inc row: (RS) K1, inc 1, patt to last 3 sts, inc 1, k2.
Cont in patt, inc in this way at each end of

You'll find it easier to evenly pick up the stitches for the ruffled edging if you place markers for each section.

You could fasten your top with a satin ribbon or use leftover yarn to knit a tie. If you prefer, you could overlap the ruffled edgings and pin them together with a brooch.

every 6th row 2 (5:5:5:5:5).
[86 (92:98:104:110:116) sts.]
Patt 35 (17:17:17:17:17) rows.

Shape armholes

Bind off 3 (4:4:5:6:6) sts at beg of next 2 rows.
3rd row: (RS) Skp, patt to last 2 sts, k2tog.
Cont in patt, dec in this way at each end of next 3 (5:5:6:7:9) RS rows. [72 (72:78:80:82:84) sts.]
Cont in patt, work 47 (45:49:49:51:51) rows.
Bind off.

LEFT FRONT

Cast on 25 (27:30:33:36:39) sts.
1st row: (RS) K4 (6:9:12:15:18), [yo, p2tog, k7] twice, yo, p2tog, m1k, k1.
2nd row: P1, m1p, p1, [yo, p2tog, p7] twice, yo, p2tog, p4 (6:9:12:15:18).
3rd row: K4 (6:9:12:15:18), [yo, p2tog, k3, yo, k2tog, k2] twice, yo, p2tog, k2, m1k, k1.
4th row: P1, m1p, p3, [yo, p2tog, p7] twice, yo, p2tog, p4 (6:9:12:15:18).
5th row: K4 (6:9:12:15:18), * yo, p2tog, k2, [yo, k2tog] twice, k1, rep from * once more, yo, p2tog, k4, m1k, k1.
6th row: P1, m1p, p5, [yo, p2tog, p7] twice, yo, p2tog, p4 (6:9:12:15:18). [31 (33:36:39:42:45) sts.]
These 6 rows set patt to match back with incs at front edge.
7th row: Patt to last 7 sts, k6, m1k, k1.
8th row: P1, m1p, p7, patt to end.
9th row: Patt to last 9 sts, k3, yo, k2tog, k2, yo, p1, k1.

10th row: P1, m1p, yo, p2tog, patt to end.
11th row: Patt to last 2 sts, k1, m1k, k1.
12th row: P1, m1p, p2, patt to end.
13th row: K2, k2tog, patt to last 4 sts, k3, m1k, k1. [37 (39:42:45:48:51) sts.]
14th row: P1, m1p, p4, patt to end.
15th row: Patt to last 6 sts, k3, yo, k2tog, m1k, k1.
16th row: P1, m1p, p6, patt to end. [40 (42:45: 48:51:54) sts.]
1st size only: Cont in patt with front edge st in St st, work 26 rows.
All other sizes: Cont in patt with front edge st in St st, work 6 rows.
Dec row: (RS) K2, k2tog, patt to end.
Cont in patt, dec in this way at beg of 10th row.
Patt 9 rows.
All sizes: [40 (40:43:46:49:52) sts.]
Inc row: (RS) K1, inc 1, patt to end.
Cont in patt, inc in this way at beg of every 6th row 2 (5:5:5:5:5). [43 (46:49:52:55:58) sts.]
Patt 35 (17:17:17:17:17) rows.

Shape armhole and neck

1st row: (RS) Bind off 3 (4:4:5:6:6) sts, patt to end.
2nd and every WS row: Patt to end.
3rd row: Skp, patt to end.
5th row: Skp, patt to last 2 sts, skp.
Working sk2p at neck edge when necessary to keep pattern correct, dec one st at each end of next 2 (4:4:5:6:8) RS rows. [33 (31:34:34: 34:33) sts.]

Cont in patt, dec one st at neck edge on next 6 (4:4:3:2:0) RS rows. [27 (27:30:31:32:33) sts.] Cont in patt, dec one st at neck edge on every 4th row 8 times. [19 (19:22:23:24:25) sts.]
Patt 1 row.
Next row: (RS) Patt to last 2 sts, p2tog. [18 (18:21:22:23:24) sts.]
Patt 1 (3:7:9:13:17) rows. Bind off.

RIGHT FRONT

Cast on 25 (27:30:33:36:39) sts.
1st row: (RS) K1, m1k, [yo, p2tog, k7] twice, yo, p2tog, k4 (6:9:12:15:18).
2nd row: P4 (6:9:12:15:18), [yo, p2tog, p7] twice, yo, p2tog, p1, m1p, p1.
3rd row: K1, m1k, k2, [yo, p2tog, k3, yo, k2tog, k2] twice, yo, p2tog, k4 (6:9:12:15:18).
4th row: P4 (6:9:12:15:18), [yo, p2tog, p7] twice, yo, p2tog, p3, m1p, p1.
5th row: K1, m1k, k4, * yo, p2tog, k2, [yo, k2tog] twice, k1, rep from * once more, yo, p2tog, k4 (6:9:12:15:18).
6th row: P4 (6:9:12:15:18), [yo, p2tog, p7] twice, yo, p2tog, p5, m1p, p1. [31 (33:36:39:42:45) sts.]
These 6 rows set patt to match back with incs at front edge.
7th row: K1, m1k, k6, patt to end.
8th row: Patt to last 8 sts, p7, m1p, p1.
9th row: K1, yo, p1, patt to end.
10th row: Patt to last 3 sts, yo, p2tog, m1p, p1.
11th row: K1, m1k, k1, yo, p2tog, patt to end.
12th row: Patt to last 3 sts, p2, m1p, p1.
13th row: K1, m1k, k3, patt to last 4 sts, skp,

k2. [37 (39:42:45:48:51) sts.]
14th row: Patt to last 5 sts, p4, m1p, p1.
15th row: K1, m1k, k1, yo, k2tog, k2, patt to end.
16th row: Patt to last 7 sts, p6, m1p, p1. [40 (42:45:48:51:54) sts.]
1st size only: Cont in patt with front edge st in St st, work 26 rows.
All other sizes: Cont in patt with front edge st in St st, work 6 rows.
Dec row: (RS) Patt to last 4 sts, skp, k2. Cont in patt, dec in this way at end of 10th row. Patt 9 rows.
All sizes: [40 (40:43:46:49:52) sts.]
Inc row: (RS) Patt to last 3 sts, inc 1, k2. Cont in patt, inc in this way at end of every 6th row 2 (5:5:5: 5:5). [43 (46:49:52:55:58) sts.]
Patt 35 (17:17:17:17:17) rows.

Shape armhole and neck

1st row: (RS) Patt to end.
2nd row: Bind off 3 (4:4:5:6:6) sts, patt to end.
3rd row: Patt to last 2 sts, k2tog. Patt 1 row.
5th row: K2tog, patt to last 2 sts, k2tog. Working k3tog at neck edge when necessary to keep pattern correct, dec one st at each end of next 2 (4:4:5:6:8) RS rows. [33 (31:34:34:34:33) sts.] Cont in patt, dec one st at neck edge on next 6 (4:4:3:2:0) RS rows. [27 (27:30:31:32:33) sts.] Cont in patt, dec one st at neck edge on every 4th row 8 times. [19 (19:22:23:24:25) sts.]
Next row: (RS) P2tog, patt to end. [18 (18:21: 22:23:24) sts.]
Patt 1 (3:7:9:13:17) rows. Bind off.

TO MAKE UP

Iron according to ball band. Matching sts, join shoulders. Join side seams.

Frill edging

With RS facing, beg at right side seam, pick up and k 22 (24:27:30:33:36) sts to start of front shaping, 18 sts around curve, 60 sts up straight edge of right front,
40 (42:45:46:49:50) sts up right front neck, 36 sts across back neck, 40 (42:45:46:49:50) sts down left front neck, 60 sts down straight edge of left front, 18 sts around curve,
22 (24:27:30:33:36) sts to left side seam, and 80 (84:88:92:96:100) sts across lower edge of back. [396 (408:424:436:452:464) sts.]
[P 1 round, k 1 round] twice. P 1 round. Work in patt.

1st round: [K2, yo, p2tog] to end.
2nd round: [K2, p2tog, yo] to end.
Work last 2 rounds 5 more times.
13th round: [K1, yo, k1, yo, p2tog] to end.
[495 (510:530:545:565:580) sts.]
14th round: [K3, p2tog, yo] to end.
15th round: [K3, yo, p2tog] to end.
16th round: * [K1, yo] 3 times, p2tog, yo, rep from * to end. [792 (816:848:872:904: 928) sts.]
17th round: [K5, p3] to end.
Picot bind-off round: K2, bind off one st, * return st to left needle, cast on 2 sts, bind off 4 sts, rep from * ending last rep bind off 2, fasten off.

Armhole edgings

With RS facing, k up 88 (92:96:100:104:108) sts around armhole.
1st round: P.
2nd round: [K2, p2] to end.
3rd round: [K1, yo, k1, p2] to end. [110 (115:120: 125:130:135) sts.]
4th and 5th rounds: [K3, p2] to end.
6th round: [K1, yo, k1, yo, k1, p1, yo, p1] to end. [176 (184:192:200:208:216) sts.]
7th round: [K5, p3] to end.
Work picot bind-off round as given for frill edging.
Iron edgings. Fold frill edging back to form collar. Try on bolero and mark where to fasten it. Sew a small loop of yarn reinforced with buttonhole, stitch on, pick up row of frill edging at marker on each front. Slip tie through loops to fasten.

This shapely jacket is very quick and easy to knit. It's made in the stockinette stitch, using a feathery yarn that makes a rich, textured fabric, so there's no need for separate bands or edgings.

Crushed Velvet Jacket

 EASY

MEASUREMENTS

To fit bust

32	34	36	38	40	42	in.
81	86	91	97	102	107	cm

Actual bust

33½	35½	37½	39½	41¼	43¼	in.
85	90	95	100	105	110	cm

Actual length

21¾	22¼	22½	23	23½	24	in.
55.5	56.5	57.5	58.5	60	61	cm

Actual sleeve length

18 in.

46 cm

In the instructions, figures are given for the smallest size first; larger sizes follow in brackets. Where only one figure is given, this applies to all sizes.

MATERIALS

- 7 (7:8:9:10:11) × 50 g (1.76 oz) balls of Crystal Palace Splash in Strawberry Soda, 9219
- Pair of US 10 (6 mm) needles
- 4 buttons

GAUGE

16 sts and 19 rows to 4 in. (10 cm) over St st on US 10 (6 mm) needles. Change needle size if necessary to obtain this gauge.

ABBREVIATIONS

[ ]—work instructions in brackets as directed. *See page 10.*

NOTES

- The needle size and gauge given are larger than usually used for Splash. This creates a soft fabric that drapes to enhance the shape of the jacket.
- Mark the RS of the fabric directly after working the first row with a safety pin or loop of contrast thread. The smooth side of St st is the right side for the garment, but it is hard to tell at a glance.
- When working the jacket, use a loop of contrast smooth thread to mark each shaping. Leave the markers in and use them to match the shapings when sewing up.
- Cast on by the knitting-off-the-thumb method (see page 11).
- Take care to gauge the first stitch firmly at the front edges to keep them neat.

To check your gauge, cast on 20 sts. Use two lengths of smooth thread in contrasting colors as markers. 1st row (RS) K2, take first marker thread between needles to WS of work, k16, take second marker thread to WS of work, k2. 2nd row P2, take marker thread to RS of work, p16, take marker thread to RS of work, p2. Cont in St st for 17 more rows, weaving marker threads between rows in this way. Bind off. To check your stitch gauge, measure between the marker threads. To check your row gauge, measure the length of the swatch, omitting cast-on and bind-off edges. If the marked area measures more than 4 in. (10 cm), try again using smaller needles; if it measures less than 4 in. (10 cm), try again using larger needles.

BACK

Cast on 68 (72:76:80:84:88) sts.
Beg k row, work in St st for 6 rows.
Dec row: (RS) K1, k2tog, k to last 3 sts, skp, k1.
Cont in St st, dec in this way at each end of every 8th row 3 times. [60 (64:68:72:76:80) sts.]
Work in St st for 9 rows.
Inc row: (RS) Inc 1, k to last 2 sts, inc 1, k1.
Cont in St st, inc in this way at each end of every 8th row 3 times. [68 (72:76:80:84:88) sts.]
Wok in St st for 5 rows.

Shape armholes

Bind off 3 sts at beg of next 2 rows.
Dec in same way as before at each end of next 3 (4:5:6:7:8) RS rows. [56 (58:60:62:64:66) sts.]
Work in St st for 29 rows. Bind off.

LEFT FRONT

Cast on 37 (39:41:43:45:47) sts.
Beg k row, work in St st for 6 rows.
Dec row: (RS) K1, k2tog, k to end.
Cont in St st, dec in this way at beg of every 8th row 3 times. [33 (35:37:39:41:43) sts.]
Work in St st for 9 rows.
Inc row: (RS) Inc 1, k to end.
Cont in St st, inc in this way at beg of every 8th row 3 times. [37 (39:41:43:45:47) sts.]
P 1 row.

Shape neck and armhole

1st dec row: (RS) K to last 3 sts, skp, k1.
Cont in St st, dec in this way at end of next RS row. P 1 row.
Next row: (RS) Bind off 3 sts, k to last 3 sts, skp, k1. [31 (33:35:37:39:41) sts.] P 1 row.
2nd dec row: (RS) K1, k2tog, k to last 3 sts, skp, k1.
Cont in St st, dec at each end of next 2 (3:4:5: 6:7) RS rows. 25 sts.
Cont in St st dec as 1st dec row at end of next 12 (11:10:10:9:8) RS rows. [13 (14:15:15:16:17) sts.]
Work in St st for 5 (7:9:9:11:13) rows. Bind off.
Place markers for 4 buttons, the top one just below the neck shaping with 3 more spaced 12 rows apart.

RIGHT FRONT

Cast on 37 (39:41:43:45:47) sts.
Beg k, work in St st for 6 rows.
Dec row: (RS) K to last 3 sts, skp, k1.
Making buttonholes opposite markers, cont in St st, dec in this way at end of every 8th row 3 times. [33 (35:37:39:41:43) sts.]
Buttonhole row: (RS) K3, yo, k2tog, k to end.
Work in St st for 9 rows.
Inc row: (RS) K to last 2 sts, inc 1, k1.
Cont in St st, inc in this way at end of every 8th row 3 times. [37 (39:41:43:45:47) sts.]
P 1 row.

It's easier to count the rows on the wrong side by running your thumbnail down the rows and counting the bumps.

To check the length by measuring rather than counting rows, the jacket should measure approximately 14¹/₂ in. (36.5 cm) to the armholes and 21³/₄ (22¹/₄:22¹/₂:23:24) in. [55.5 (56.5:57.5:58.5:60:61) cm] to the shoulders. Make sure that you spread the garment out to its full width before measuring or you could find that your measurements are not accurate.

Shape neck and armhole

1st dec row: K1, k2tog, k to end.

Cont in St st, dec in this way at beg of next 2 RS rows.

Next row: (WS) Bind off 3 sts, p to end. [31 (33:35:37:39:41) sts.]

2nd dec row: (RS) K1, k2tog, k to last 3 sts, skp, k1.

Cont in St st, dec at each end of next 2 (3:4:5:6:7) RS rows. [25 sts.]

Cont in St st dec as 1st dec row at beg of next 12 (11:10:10:9:8) RS rows. [13 (14:15:15:16:17) sts.]

St st 5 (7:9:9:11:13) rows. Bind off.

SLEEVES

Cast on 33 (33:35:35:37:37) sts.

Beg k, work in St st for 8 (6:6:4:8:8) rows.

Inc row: (RS) Inc 1, k to last 2 sts, inc 1, k1.

Cont in St st, inc in this way at each end of every 8th (8th:8th:8th:6th:6th) row (8 (9:9:10:10:11) times. [51 (53:55:57:59:61) sts.]

Work in St st for 15 (9:9:3:19:13) rows.

Shape top

Bind off 3 sts at beg of next 2 rows.

Dec in same way as before at each end of next 11 (12:13:14:15:16) RS rows. [23 sts.] P 1 row. Bind off.

TO MAKE UP

Matching sts, join shoulders. Set in sleeves. Join side and sleeve seams. Sew on buttons.

Turn heads when you turn around in this sophisticated slimline sweater. Highlight the plunging style by wearing an opera-length necklace at the back.

V-Back Sweater

 INTERMEDIATE

MEASUREMENTS

To fit bust

32	34	36	38	40	42	in.
81	86	91	97	102	107	cm

Actual measurement across front

16	17^1/$_4$	18^1/$_2$	19^3/$_4$	20^1/$_2$	21^1/$_2$	in.
41	44	47	50	52	55	cm

Actual length

20	20^1/$_2$	20^3/$_4$	21^1/$_4$	21^1/$_4$	22	in.
51	52	53	54	54	56	cm

Actual sleeve length
12^1/$_2$ in.
32 cm

In the instructions, figures are given for the smallest size first; larger sizes follow in brackets. Where only one figure is given, this applies to all sizes.

MATERIALS

- 7 (7:8:8:8:9) × 50 g (1.76 oz) balls of Debbie Bliss Cathay in purple, 12
- Pair each of US 3 (3 mm) and US 5 (3^3/$_4$ mm) needles
- US 5 (3^3/$_4$ mm) circular needle, 39^1/$_2$ in. (100 cm) long

GAUGE

22 sts and 30 rows to 4 in. (10 cm) over St st on US 5 (3^3/$_4$ mm) needles.

ABBREVIATIONS

See page 10.

FRONT

Using US 3 (3 mm) needles, cast on 88 (94:100:106:112:118) sts.
1st rib row: (RS) P1, * k2, p1; rep from * to end.
2nd rib row: K1, *p2, k1; rep from * to end.
Rep these 2 rows 6 times more. Change to US 5 (3^3/$_4$ mm) needles. Beg k row, work in St st for 4 rows.
1st dec row: (RS) K1, skp, k to last 3 sts, k2tog, k1. **
Cont to dec in this way at each end of every foll 6th row 4 times. [78 (84:90:96:102:108) sts.]
Beg and ending p row, work in St st for 7 rows.
1st inc row: (RS) K2, m1, k to last 2 sts, m1, k2.
Cont to inc in this way at each end of every foll 8th row 6 times. [92 (98:104:110:116:122) sts.]
Beg and ending p row, work in St st for 5 rows straight.

Shape armholes

Bind off 3 (3:3:4:4:4) sts at beg of next 2 rows.
Next row: (RS) K1, skp, k to last 3 sts, k2tog, k1.
Cont to dec in this way at each end of next 8 (9:10:10:11:12) RS rows. [68 (72:76:80:84:88) sts.]
Beg and ending p row, work in St st for 17 (17:19:19:19:21) rows straight.

Instead of slipping "waiting" stitches onto a spare needle, leave them on a length of contrasting yarn for lightness and flexibility when you work.

Neck shaping

1st row: (RS) K21 (23:25:27:28:30) sts, turn.
Cont on these sts only for first side and leave rem sts on a spare needle.

2nd row: P3, k1, p to end.

3rd row: K to last 6 sts, skp, p1, k3.
Rep last 2 rows twice more. [18 (20:22:24:25: 27) sts.]
Patt 10 (10:10:12:12:12) rows straight—patt means working one stitch rib 3 sts in from neck edge.
Bind off.

Next row: (RS) Slip center 26 (26:26:26:28: 28) sts onto a spare needle, k to end.

Next row: P to last 4 sts, k1, p3.

Next row: K3, p1, k2tog, k to end.
Complete to match first side.

BACK

Using US 3 (3 mm) needles, cast on 82 (88:94:100:106:112) sts.
Work as front to **. Cont to dec in this way at each end of every foll 6th row 4 times more, so ending with with a RS row. [72 (78:84:90: 96:102) sts.]

Next row: P32 (35:38:41:44:47), k1, p6, k1, p32 (35:38:41:44:47).

Shape center and side

1st row: (RS) K30 (33:36:39:42:45), skp, p1, k3, turn.
Cont on these sts only for first side and leave rem sts on a spare needle.

2nd and WS rows: P3, k1, p to end.

3rd row: K to last 6 sts, skp, p1, k3.

5th row: As 3rd row.

7th row: K2, m1, k to last 4 sts, p1, k3.
Cont to inc in this way at side edge on every foll 8th row 6 times more while **at the same time** dec as before at center edge on next RS row and every foll 4th row until a total of 7 (7:8:8:9:9) dec rows has been completed at center edge, then dec at center edge on every foll 6th row 6 (6:5:5:5:5) times. [30 (33:36:39:41:44) sts.]
Patt 3 (3:5:5:1:1) rows straight, so ending with a WS row.

Shape armhole

Bind off 3 (3:3:4:4:4) sts at beg of next row.

Next RS row: K1, skp, k to last 4 sts, p1, k3.
Cont to dec in this way at beg of next 8 (9:10: 10:11:12) RS rows. [18 (20:22:24:25:27) sts.]
Patt straight until work matches front to shoulder, so ending with a WS row. Bind off.

Next row: (RS) Rejoin yarn to inner end of rem sts, k3, p1, k2tog, k to end.
Complete to match first side, working one more row to armhole and working decs as k2tog.

SLEEVES

With US 3 (3 mm) needles, cast on 46 (49:52:52:55: 58) sts.
Rib 14 rows as front. Change to US 5 (3³/4 mm) needles. Beg k row, work in St st for 6 (6:6:4:4:4) rows straight.

Next row: (RS) K2, m1, k to last 2 sts, m1, k2.
Cont to inc in this way at each end of every foll
10th (10th:10th:8th:8th:8th) row 7 (7:7:9:9:9)
times. [62 (65:68:72:75:78) sts.]
Cont straight until work measures 12¹/₂ in.
(32 cm), ending p row.

Shape top

Bind off 3 (3:3:4:4:4) sts at beg of next 2 rows.
Next row: (RS) K1, skp, k to last 3 sts, k2tog, k1.
Cont to dec in this way at each end of next
8 (9:10:10:11:12) RS rows. [38 (39:40:42:43:
44) sts.]
Dec as before at each end of every foll 4th row
4 times. [30 (31:32:34:35:36) sts.]
Bind off 2 sts at beg of next 6 rows. Bind off
rem 18 (19:20:22:23:24) sts purlwise.

NECK EDGING

Join right shoulder seam.
With RS facing and using US 5 (3³/₄ mm)
circular needle, pick up and k14 (14:14:16:16:16)
sts down left front neck, k26 (26:26:26:28:28)
sts from front neck, pick up and k14 (14:14:
16:16:16) sts up right front neck, 86 (88:90:
92:92:96) sts down right back and 86 (88:90:
92:92:96) sts up left back. [226 (230:234:242:
244:252) sts.]
Turn and bind off knitwise, working skp in
last 2 sts before center V at back and k2tog in
first 2 sts after center V.

TO MAKE UP

Join left shoulder seam. Iron according
to ball band. Set in sleeves. Join side and
sleeve seams.

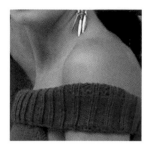

Show off your shoulders and look like a film star when you wear this slinky top.

Off-the-Shoulder Top

 EASY

MEASUREMENTS

To fit bust

32	34	36	38	40	42	in.
81	86	91	97	102	107	cm

Actual bust

$32^{1}/_{4}$	$33^{3}/_{4}$	$35^{3}/_{4}$	38	40	$41^{3}/_{4}$	in.
82	86	91	97	102	106	cm

Actual length to underarm

$15^{3}/_{4}$	$15^{3}/_{4}$	$15^{3}/_{4}$	$15^{3}/_{4}$	$15^{3}/_{4}$	$15^{3}/_{4}$	in.
40	40	40	40	40	40	cm

In the instructions, figures are given for the smallest size first; larger sizes follow in brackets. Where only one figure is given, this applies to all sizes.

MATERIALS

- 6 (7:7:7:8:8) x 50 g (1.76 oz) balls Debbie Bliss Cashmerino Aran in blue, 208
- Pair each of US 6 (4 mm) and US 8 (5 mm) knitting needles
- US 6 (4 mm) circular needle, $31^{1}/_{2}$ in. (80 cm)

GAUGE

18 sts and 24 rows to 4 in. (10 cm) over St st on US 8 (5 mm) needles.

ABBREVIATIONS

[ ]—work instructions in brackets as directed. *See also page 10.*

FRONT

Using US 6 (4 mm) needles, cast on 90 (94:98:106:110:114) sts.
1st rib row: (RS) K2, * p2, k2; rep from * to end.
2nd rib row: P2, * k2, p2; rep from * to end.
Rep these 2 rows 8 times more, then work 1st rib row again.
Next row: (WS) Rib 2 (2:2:6:6:6), [k2tog, rib 6] 5 times, k2tog, rib 2 (6:10:10:14:18), [k2tog, rib 6] 5 times, k2tog, rib 2 (2:2:6:6:6). [78 (82:86:94:98:102) sts.]
Change to US 8 (5 mm) needles. Beg k row, work in St st for 4 rows.
1st dec row: (RS) K21 (22:23:25:26:27), k2tog, k32 (34:36:40:42:44), skp, k 21 (22:23:25:26:27). Beg p row, work in St st for 3 rows.
2nd dec row: (RS) K21 (22:23:25:26:27), k2tog, k30 (32:34:38:40:42), skp, k21 (22:23:25:26:27).
Cont to dec in this way, working 2 sts less between each pair of decs, on every foll 4th row until a total of 7 dec rows has been completed. [64 (68:72:80:84:88) sts.]
Beg and ending p row, work in St st for 7 (7:7:9:9:9) rows straight.
1st inc row: (RS) K21 (22:23:25:26:27), m1, k to last 21 (22:23:25:26:27) sts, m1, k 21 (22:23:25:26:27).

Cont to inc in this way on every foll 8th (8th:8th:10th:10th:10th) row 4 (4:4:3:3:3) times. [74 (78:82:88:92:96) sts.] Beg and ending p row, work in St st for 11 rows straight.

Shape armholes
Bind off 6 (6:6:7:7:7) sts at beg of next 2 rows.
Next row: (RS) K2, k2tog, k to last 4 sts, skp, k2. **
Cont to dec in this way on next 6 (7:8:9:10:11) RS rows, so ending with a RS row. [48 (50:52: 54:56:58) sts.] Leave sts on a spare needle.

BACK
As front to **.
Cont to dec in this way on next 2 (3:4:5:6:7) RS rows. [56 (58:60:62:64:66) sts.]
Work in St st for 14 rows straight, so ending with a RS row. Do not break yarn.

CUFF
Sl sts of back onto US 6 (4 mm) circular needle, using attached yarn and with WS facing, cast on by cable method (see note right) 26 (30:34:38:42:44) sts, turn and with RS facing, k48 (50:52:54:56:58) sts of front, turn, cast on 26 (30:34:38:42:44) sts, turn, k56 (58:60:62:64:66) sts of back. [156 (168:180: 192:204:212) sts.]

With RS facing, work in rounds.
1st round: * K2, p2; rep from * to end.
Rep this round 12 times more.
14th round: * Inc 1, k1, p2; rep from * to end.
15th round: * K3, p2; rep from * to end.
Rep last round 14 times more.
Bind off loosely in rib.

ARMHOLE EDGING
Join side seams.
With RS facing and using US 6 (4 mm) circular needle, pick up and k22 (24:26:28:32) sts around left back armhole, one st from side seam and 18 (20:22:24:28) sts around left front armhole. [41 (45:49:53:61) sts.]
Bind off knitwise.
Work right armhole to match.

TO MAKE UP
Iron St st according to instructions on ball band. Catch down ends of armhole edging. Turn cuff in half to RS.

*Cable cast-on for cuff: *k in first st on lefthand needle but do not slip it off, put the new loop from the right needle onto the left needle; rep from *, inserting right needle between first and 2nd sts to make each new st.*

Carry all of your party essentials in this easy-to-make envelope-style beaded clutch bag.

Beaded Clutch Bag

MEASUREMENTS

Actual width
9¹/₂ in.
24 cm

Actual height
5¹/₂ in.
14 cm

MATERIALS

- 2 × 50 g (1.76 oz) hanks of Debbie Bliss Pure Silk in turquoise, 07
- Pair of US 3 (3¹/₄ mm) knitting needles
- 2,256 medium glass seed beads (size 5/0)
- Heavy, iron-on interlining—one piece 9¹/₂ × 10¹/₂ in. (24 × 27 cm), one piece 9¹/₂ × 17 in. (24 × 43 cm)
- Lining fabric—one piece 10¹/₂ × 18 in. (27 × 46 cm) and two pieces 3¹/₄ × 5 in. (8.5 × 13 cm)
- Matching sewing thread and a sharp needle
- Press stud or magnetic bag catch (optional)
- Round pierced metal brooch form and assorted beads (optional)

GAUGE

21 sts and 30 rows to 4 in. (10 cm) over beaded reverse St st, 25 sts and 35 rows to 4 in. (10 cm) over St st on US 3 (3¹/₄ mm) needles. Change needle size if necessary to obtain these gauges.

The medium-sized seed beads used for the bag are often called size 5 or 5/0. They are colored glass with a shiny, silvery lining.
You can use any beads for your bag: pearly, metallic, or clear glass. You could even work in stripes of different colors. Just make sure that you choose beads with a hole large enough to thread them onto the yarn.
It is practical to thread between 300 and 500 beads onto the yarn at a time. When you don't have enough beads left to work a row, cut the yarn at the beginning of a row, add more beads, and rejoin the yarn. Never join in new yarn in the middle of a row.

ABBREVIATIONS

B—bring a bead up close to the work;
[ ]—work instructions in brackets as directed.
See also page 10.

NOTES

- This kind of knitting is easy to do because the beads lie between the stitches.
- The bag is knitted using smaller needles than usual for Debbie Bliss Pure Silk to give a firm fabric.
- You only need to thread beads onto the yarn for the bag flap; the rest of the bag is knitted without beads.
- Check the size of your bag before cutting the lining and interlining. If your gauge is not correct, your bag will be a different size and you will need to adjust the measurements.

FLAP

Using beaded yarn, cast on 51 sts.
K 1 row.
1st row: (RS) P2, [B, p1] to last st, p1.
2nd row: K2, [B, k1] to last st, k1.
These 2 rows form beaded reverse St st.
Work 45 more rows. Bind off loosely.

BACK AND FRONT

Using yarn without beads, cast on 60 sts.
Beg k row, work in St st for 97 rows. Bind off knitwise.

SIDE PANELS

(Make 2) Using yarn without beads, cast on 14 sts. Beg k row, work in St st for 35 rows. Bind off knitwise.

TO MAKE UP

Join bind-off edge of flap to bind-off edge of back and front. Leaving one stitch free at each side and 2 rows free at cast-on edge, fuse the $9^1/2 \times 10^1/2$ in. (24 × 27 cm) piece of interlining to the back and front of bag. Using mattress stitch and taking one stitch into seam, leaving 2 rows at cast-on edge of back and front of bag free, set in side panels. Leaving $1/2$ in. (1.5 cm) of lining free all around, fuse the $9^1/2 \times 17$ in. (24 × 43 cm), piece of iron-on interlining to the $10^1/2 \times 18$ in. (27 × 46 cm) piece of lining fabric. With raw edge of seam allowance on same side as interlining and leaving approximately $6^1/4$ in. (16 cm) free at one end for flap lining, set in lining side pieces. Iron in all seam allowances.
Placing interlinings together, insert lining into bag. If using a magnetic bag catch or other catch, it may be necessary to insert it at this stage. Fix according to manufacturer's instructions. Slip stitch lining in place. Catch tops of side panels together.
If not using a bag catch, sew press stud on front and flap of bag.
For the optional decoration, stitch beads to the pierced metal form and sew on bag.

The type of heavyweight iron-on interlining that you need is often labeled as suitable for collar stiffening or for tie-backs, pelmets, and furnishings.

If you can't find a heavyweight iron-on interlining, you could use a non-iron interlining and hold it in place with stitching.

A size 10 quilting needle makes small neat stitches when sewing the lining, but you could use any type of sharp needle, or, if you prefer, a sewing machine.

This flattering, wispy little top won't keep you warm but will add appealing glamor to any outfit.

Skimpy Shrug

 ADVANCED

MEASUREMENTS

Stretches to fit bust

32	34	36	38	in.
81	86	91	97	cm

Actual bust

30^1/$_2$	33^1/$_4$	35^1/$_2$	38^1/$_4$	in.
77.5	84.5	90.5	97.5	cm

Actual length

13	13^1/$_2$	15	15^1/$_2$	in.
33	34	38	39	cm

Actual sleeve length

10 in.

25 cm

In the instructions, figures are given for the smallest size first; larger sizes follow in brackets. Where only one figure is given, this applies to all sizes.

MATERIALS

- 3 (3:4:4) × 25 g (0.88 oz) balls of Rowan Kid Silk Haze in Jelly, 597
- Pair of US 7 (4^1/$_2$ mm) needles
- US E/4 (3.5 mm) crochet hook

GAUGE

24 sts and 24 rows to 4 in. (10 cm) over blackberry stitch on US 7 (4^1/$_2$ mm) needles. Change needle size if necessary to obtain this gauge.

ABBREVIATIONS

dc—double crochet; [ ]—work instructions in brackets as directed. *See also page 10.*

NOTE

- To cast on at the end of a row, loop yarn around left thumb and slip loop onto right needle for each stitch.

BACK

Cast on 95 (99:103:107) sts.

1st and 3rd rows: (RS) P.

2nd row: P1, * [k1, p1, k1] in next st, p3tog, rep from * to last 2 sts, [k1, p1, k1] in next st, p1. [97 (101:105:109) sts.]

4th row: P1, * p3tog, [k1, p1, k1] in next st, rep from * to last 4 sts, p3tog, p1. [95 (99:103:107) sts.] These 4 rows form blackberry st patt. Work 28 (28:32:32) more rows, so ending with a 4th patt row.

Shape armholes

1st row: (RS) Bind off 5 (5:9:9) sts purlwise, p to end.

2nd row: Bind off 5 (5:9:9) sts knitwise, one st on right needle, beg p3tog, patt as 4th row to end. [83 (87:83:87) sts.]

The needle size is larger than commonly used for Kid Silk Haze to achieve the lacy effect. You may find it easier to knit with the weight of the right needle supported under the right arm.

The blackberry stitch pattern is worked by alternately making three stitches from one and taking three stitches together. Where there is an increase group at each end of a row, the stitch count increases by two; where there is a decrease group at each end of a row, the stitch count decreases by two; where there is an increase group at one end and a decrease group at the other end of a row, the stitch count remains constant. Stitch counts for each change are given throughout.

3rd row: P2tog, p to last 2 sts, p2tog.
[81 (85:81:85) sts.]
4th row: Work as given for 4th patt row.
[79 (83:79:83) sts.]
Work 3rd and 4th rows 2(2:0:0) more times.
[71 (75:79:83) sts.]
Patt 40 (42:52:54) rows straight. [71 (77:79:85) sts.] Bind off.

RIGHT FRONT

Cast on 3 sts.
1st row: (RS) P.
2nd row: P1, [k1, p1, k1] in next st, p1. [5 sts.]
3rd, 5th, 7th, and 9th rows: P1, yo, p to last st, yo, p1.
4th row: P1, [k1, p1, k1] in next st, p3tog, [k1, p1, k1] in next st, p1. [9 sts.]
6th row: P1, * [k1, p1, k1] in next st, p3tog, rep from * once, [k1, p1, k1] in next st, p1. [13 sts.]
8th row: P1, * [k1, p1, k1] in next st, p3tog, rep from * twice, [k1, p1, k1] in next st, p1, [17 sts.]
10th row: P1, * [k1, p1, k1] in next st, p3tog, rep from * 3 times, [k1, p1, k1] in next st, p1. [21 sts.]
11th and 13th rows: P.
12th row: P1, * p3tog, [k1, p1, k1] in next st, rep from * 3 times, p3tog, p1. [19 sts.]
14th row: P1, * [k1, p1, k1] in next st, p3tog, rep from * 3 times, [k1, p1, k1] in next st, p1. [21 sts.]
Work 11th to 14th rows 4 more times. [21 sts.]

Shape front

1st inc row: (RS) P1, yo, p to last st, yo, p1.
[23 sts.]

2nd inc row: P1, * [k1, p1, k1] in next st, p3tog, rep from * to last 2 sts, [k1, p1, k1] in next st, p1.
[25 sts.]
Work 1st and 2nd inc rows 4 more times.
[41 sts **.]

Shape neck

Next row: P1, yo, p to end. 42 sts.
Next row: P1, * p3tog, [k1, p1, k1] in next st, rep from * to last st, p1. [42 sts.]
Keeping patt at lower edge straight, inc by working p1, yo at neck edge on next 4 (5:6:7) RS rows. [50 (51:54:55) sts.]
Patt 1 row. [50 (53:54:57) sts.] Do not turn.

Shape shoulder

Cast on 28 (29:28:29) sts. [78 (82:82:86) sts.]
Noting that st count is constant, beg p row, patt 14 (18:22:26) rows, so ending with a WS row.

Shape armhole

Next row: (RS) Bind off 37 (40:42:44) sts purlwise, p to end. [41 (42:40:42) sts.]
Next row: Patt, ending, p3tog, p1. [40 (42:38: 42) sts.]
Keeping patt at lower edge straight, dec by working p2tog at beg of next 4 (4:2:2) RS rows and ending WS rows p3tog, p1. [33 (34:36: 38) sts.]
Noting that st count for 1st and 3rd sizes varies by 2 sts, patt 3 (3:7:7) rows. Bind off.

LEFT FRONT

Work as given for right front to **.

Shape neck

Next row: P to last st, yo, p1. 42 sts.
Next row: P1, * [k1, p1, k1] in next st, p3tog, rep from * to last st, p1. [42 sts.]
Keeping patt at lower edge straight, inc by ending next 4 (5:6:7) RS rows yo, p1. [50 (51:54:55) sts.]
Patt 1 row. [50 (53:54:57) sts.]

Shape shoulder

Next row: P to end, do not turn, cast on 28 (29:28:29) sts. [78 (82:82:86 sts.]
Noting that st count is constant, patt 14 (18:22:26) rows, so ending with a p row.

Shape armhole

Next row: (WS) Bind off 37 (40:41:44) sts, one st on right needle, beg p3tog, patt to end. [39 (42:39:42) sts.]
Keeping patt at lower edge straight, dec by working p2tog at end of next 4 (4:2:2) RS rows and beg WS rows p1, p3tog. [33 (34:37:38) sts.]
Noting that st count for 1st and 3rd sizes varies by 2 sts, patt 3 (3:7:7) rows. Bind off.

SLEEVES

Cast on 99 (99:111:111) sts.
Patt 8 rows as given for back, so ending with a 4th patt row.
1st dec row: (RS) P2tog, p to last 2 sts, p2tog.

2nd dec row: Work as given for 4th patt row.
Alternating st count between 97 (97:109:109)
and 95 (95:107:107) sts, patt 8 rows.
Work 1st and 2nd dec rows again.
Alternating st count between 93 (93:105:105)
and 91 (91:103:103) sts, patt 8 rows.
Work 1st and 2nd dec rows again.
Alternating st count between 89 (89:101:101)
and 87 (87:99:99) sts, patt 8 rows.
Work 1st and 2nd dec rows again.
Alternating st count between 85 (85:97:97)
and 83 (83:95:95) sts, patt 20 rows. [83 (83:95:
95) sts.]

Shape top

1st row: (RS) Bind off 5 (5:9:9) sts purlwise,
p to end.
2nd row: Bind off 5 (5:9:9) sts knitwise, one st
on right needle, beg p3tog, patt to end.
[71 (71:75:75) sts.]
3rd row: P2tog, p to last 2 sts, p2tog.
4th row: Work as 4th patt row.
Work 3rd and 4th rows 10 more times.
[27 (27:31:31) sts.]
Bind off 4 sts at beg of next 4 rows. [11 (11:15:
15) sts.] Bind off.

TO MAKE UP

Matching sts, join shoulders. Set in sleeves.
Join side and sleeve seams.

Edging

Using crochet hook and with RS facing, join
yarn at right front side seam, skipping sts or
row-ends where necessary to keep edge neat,
work 63 (67:71:75) dc along lower edge to
center of tie, 71 (75:79:83) dc along tie and up
right front neck, 35 (35:37:37) dc across back
neck, 71 (75:79:83) dc down left front neck to
center of tie, 63 (67:71:75) dc along tie and
lower edge of left front and 77 (81:85:89) dc
across back, join in 1st dc with a slip st, turn.
[380 (400:422:442) dc.]
Work 1dc in each dc around edge, slip st in 1st
dc, fasten off.

Cuff edgings

Working into each st to flare the edge, join
yarn at seam and work to match edging.

Feel nostalgic in this shapely little camisole top with a front cable panel that suggests laced-up ribbon.

Cabled Camisole

MEASUREMENTS

To fit bust

32	34	36	38	40	42	in.
81	86	91	97	102	107	cm

Actual bust

30³/₄	32³/₄	35	37¹/₂	39¹/₂	41¹/₄	in.
78	83	89	95	100	105	cm

Actual length to underarm

11³/₄	11³/₄	12	12	12¹/₄	12¹/₄	in.
30	30	30.5	30.5	31	31	cm

In the instructions, figures are given for the smallest size first; larger sizes follow in brackets. Where only one figure is given, this applies to all sizes.

MATERIALS

- 4 (4:5:5:6:6) × 50 g (1.76 oz) balls of Debbie Bliss Cathay in duck egg, 08
- Pair each of US 3 (3¹/₄ mm) and US 5 (3³/₄ mm) knitting needles
- Cable needle

GAUGE

22 sts and 30 rows to 4 in. (10 cm) over St st on US 5 (3³/₄ mm) needles.

ABBREVIATIONS

c3b—sl one st onto cable needle and hold at back, k2 then k1 from cable needle; **c3f**—sl 2 sts onto cable needle and hold at front, k1 then k2 from cable needle; **tbl**   through back of loops. *See also page 10.*

NOTE

The panels of cable used in this design are explained both as charts (see pages 58 and 60) and as row-by-row instructions so that you can choose your preferred method of following the stitch pattern.

Panel A
Worked over 12 sts.
1st row: (RS) P1, k2, c3b, c3f, k2, p1.
2nd and WS rows: P.
3rd row: P1, k1, c3b, k2, c3f, k1, p1.
5th row: P1, c3b, k4, c3f, p1.
7th row: P1, c3f, k4, c3b, p1.
9th row: P1, k1, c3f, k2, c3b, k1, p1.
11th row: P 1, k2, c3f, c3b, k2, p1.
12th row: P.

Panel B
Worked over 24 sts.
1st row: (RS) P1, k2, c3b, k3, c3b, c3f, k3, c3f, k2, p1.
2nd and WS rows: P.
3rd row: P1, k1, c3b, k3, c3b, k2, c3f, k3, c3f, k1, p1.

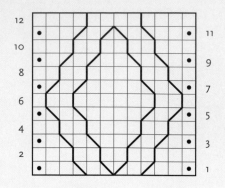

KEY CHART A

☐ *K on RS rows, p on WS rows*

⊡ *P on RS rows*

◩◪ *Sl one st onto cable needle and hold at back, k2 then k1 from cable needle (c3b)*

◤◥ *Sl 2 sts onto cable needle and hold at front, k1 then k2 from cable needle (c3f)*

Note: Read all odd-numbered RS rows from right to left.

5th row: P1, c3b, k3, c3b, k4, c3f, k3, c3f, p1.

7th row: P1, k5, c3b, k3, c3b, c3f, k5, p1.

9th row: P1, k4, c3b, k3, c3b, k2, c3f, k4, p1.

11th row: P1, k3, c3b, k3, c3b, k4, c3f, k3, p1.

12th row: P.

BACK

Using US 3 (3¼ mm) needles, cast on 78 (84:90:96:102:108) sts.

Beg k row, work in St st for 4 rows. Change to US 5 (3¾ mm) needles and patt:

1st row: (RS) K15 (18:20:23:25:28), patt 12 sts of 1st row of chart A or 1st row of panel A, k24 (24:26:26:28:28), patt 12 sts of 1st row of chart A or 1st row of panel A, k15 (18:20:23:25:28).

2nd and WS rows: P.

3rd row: K15 (18:20:23:25:28), patt 12 sts of 3rd row of chart A or 3rd row of panel A, k24 (24:26:26:28:28), patt 12 sts of 3rd row of chart A or 3rd row of panel A, k15 (18:20:23:25:28).

5th row: K2, skp, k11 (14:16:19:21:24), patt 12 sts of 5th row of chart A or 5th row of panel A, k24 (24:26:26:28:28), patt 12 sts of 5th row of chart A or 5th row of panel A, k11 (14:16:19:21:24), k2tog, k2.

7th row: K14 (17:19:22:24:27), patt 12 sts of 7th row of chart A or 7th row of panel A, k24(24:26:26:28:28), patt 12 sts of 7th row of chart A or 7th row of panel A, k14 (17:19:22:24:27).

9th row: K2, skp, k10 (13:15:18:20:23), patt 12 sts of 9th row of chart A or 9th row of panel A, k24 (24:26:26:28:28), patt 12 sts of 9th row of chart A or 9th row of panel A, k10 (13:15:18:20:23), k2tog, k2.

11th row: K13 (16:18:21:23:26), patt 12 sts of 11th row of chart A or 11th row of panel A, k24 (24:26:26:28:28), patt 12 sts of 11th row of chart A or 11th row of panel A, k13 (16:18:21:23:26).

12th row: P.

These 12 rows form patt. Rep 1st–12th rows while **at the same time** dec as before at each end of next row and every foll 4th row, working one st less after first dec and one st less before 2nd dec each time, until 6 dec rows have been completed. [66 (72:78:84:90:96) sts.]

Patt 19 rows straight, so ending with a WS row.

45th row: K3, m1, patt to last 3 sts, m1, k3. Cont to inc in this way at each end of every foll 6th row until 4 inc rows have been completed. [74 (80:86:92:98:104) sts.]

Cont to inc at each end of every foll 4th row until a total of 10 inc rows has been completed. [86 (92:98:104:110:116) sts.]

Patt 3 (3:5:5:7:7) rows straight, so ending with a WS row.

Shape armholes and neck

** Keeping patt correct, bind off 6 (7:7:8:8:9) sts at beg of next 2 rows.

Next row: (RS) K2, skp, patt to last 4 sts, k2tog, k2.

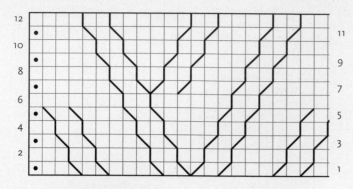

KEY CHART B

□ *K on RS rows, p on WS rows*

• *P on RS rows*

◿◿ *Sl 1 st onto cable needle and hold at back, k2 then k1 from cable needle (c3b)*

◺◺ *Sl 2 sts onto cable needle and hold at front, k1 then k2 from cable needle (c3f)*

Note Read all odd-numbered RS rows from right to left.

Cont to dec in this way on next 4 (4:6:6:8:8) RS rows. *** [64 (68:70:74:76:80) sts.]
P one row.

Next row: (RS) K8 (10:10:12:12:14) sts, turn.
Cont on these sts only for first side and leave rem sts on a spare needle.

Next row: P2tog tbl, p to end.

Next row: K to last 2 sts, skp.
Rep last 2 rows 2 (3:3:4:4:5) times more.
P2tog tbl. Fasten off.

Next row: (RS) Rejoin yarn to inner end of rem sts; working p1, k1, skp, k4, k2tog, k1, p1, k24 (24:26:26:28:28), p1, k1, skp, k4, k2tog, k1, p1, bind off center 48 (48:50:50:52:52) sts; k rem 8 (10:10:12:12:14) sts.

Next row: P to last 2 sts, p2tog.

Next row: K2tog, k to end.
Rep last 2 rows 2 (3:3:4:4:5) times more.
P2tog. Fasten off.

FRONT

Using US 3 (3¼ mm) needles, cast on 82 (88:94:100:106:112) sts.

Beg k row, St st 4 rows. Change to US 5 (3¾ mm) needles and patt:

1st row: (RS) K15 (18:20:23:25:28), patt 12 sts of 1st row of chart A or panel A, k2 (2:3:3:4:4), patt 24 sts of 1st row of chart B or panel B, k2 (2:3:3:4:4), patt 12 sts of 1st row of chart A or panel A, k15 (18:20:23:25:28).

2nd and WS rows: P.

3rd row: K15 (18:20:23:25:28), patt 12 sts of 3rd row of chart A or panel A, k2 (2:3:3:4:4), patt

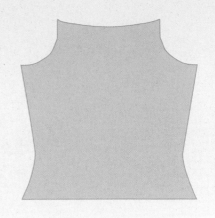

24 sts of 3rd row of chart B or panel B, k2 (2:3:3:4:4), patt 12 sts of 3rd row of chart A or panel A, k 15 (18:20:23:25:28).

Cont to patt as set, dec one st as for back at each end of next RS row and every foll 4th row until 6 dec rows has been completed. [70 (76:82:88:94:100) sts.]

Patt 19 rows straight, so ending with a WS row. Inc as for back at each end of next and every foll 6th row until 4 inc rows have been completed. [78 (84:90:96:102:108) sts.]

Cont to inc at each end of every foll 4th row until a total of 10 inc rows have been completed.

[90 (96:102:108:114:120) sts.]

Patt 3 (3:5:5:7:7) rows straight, so ending with a WS row.

Shape armholes and neck

As back from ** to ***. [68 (72:74:78:80:84) sts.]
P one row.

Next row: (RS) K8 (10:10:12:12:14) sts, turn. Cont on these sts only for first side and leave rem sts on a spare needle.

Next row: P2tog tbl, p to end.

Next row: K to last 2 sts, skp.

Rep last 2 rows 2 (3:3:4:4:5) times more.

P2tog tbl. Fasten off.

Next row: (RS) Rejoin yarn to inner end of rem sts; working p1, k1, skp, k4, k2tog, k1, p1, k2 (2:3:3:4:4), p1, k1, skp, k4, skp, k4, k2tog, k4, k2tog, k1, p1, k2 (2:3:3:4:4), p1, k1, skp, k4, k2tog, k1, p1, bind off center 52 (52:54:54:56:56)

sts, k rem 8 (10:10:12:12:14) sts.
Complete as 2nd side of back.

BAND

Join side seams, reversing seams for first 4 rows at cast-on edge.

Using US 3 (3¹/₄ mm) needles, cast on 6 sts.

1st row: (RS) P1, k4, p1.

2nd row: P.

3rd row: P1, sl next 2 sts onto cable needle and hold at back, k2 then k2 from cable needle, p1.

4th row: P.

These 4 rows form patt. Rep 1st–4th rows until band, slightly stretched, fits around back neck, over shoulder, around front neck and over shoulder. Bind off.

ARMHOLE EDGING

With RS facing and using US 5 (3³/₄ mm) needles, pick up and k21 (23:26:28:31:33) sts around left back armhole and 21 (23:26:28:31:33) sts around left front armhole.
42 (46:52:56:62:66) sts.
Bind off knitwise.
Work right armhole to match.

TO MAKE UP

Iron lightly according to ball band.
Join ends of band and seam to the back, sew to back and front neck.

SHIMMER AND SHINE

Go for full-on nighttime glamor or glitter in the daytime
with shimmering metallic knits. Show off your shoulders
in a skinny garnet top, sparkle in a cropped gold vest, cover
up in style with a sophisticated pewter jacket, or go for all-
over shine in a copper sequin tank top. Slip into a dreamy,
creamy cardigan decorated with the subtle sheen of pearly
beads, take on an urban look with studs and stones on
denim, and accessorize your outfit with a glittering brushed
wrap or sequin-scattered scarf.

There are lots of different ways you can wind, twist, or knot this long narrow scarf glinting with scattered sequins.

Skinny Scarf

EASY

MEASUREMENTS
1¹/₄ in. (3 cm) wide × 79 in (200 cm) long, excluding fringe

MATERIALS
- 25 g (0.88 oz) ball of Rowan Kid Silk Haze in Candy Girl, 606
- Pair of US 3 (3¹/₄ mm) knitting needles
- Flat ¹/₂ in. (10 mm) sequins in pink and purple
- Sewing needle with a narrow oval eye
- Medium-sized crochet hook

GAUGE
24 sts and 30 rows to 4 in. (10 cm) over St st on US 3 (3¹/₄ mm) needles.

ABBREVIATIONS
sq1—slide a sequin along the yarn and hold it tight against the righthand needle, insert righthand needle in next st, take yarn round righthand needle to make a k st, then push sequin through the st to RS as it is being slipped off the needle, tighten yarn if necessary before proceeding to next st. *See also page 10.*

Use sewing needle to thread sequins directly onto yarn, alternating colors.
Cast on 18 sts.
Beg k row, work in St st for 4 rows.

Now patt as follows:
5th row: (RS) K7, sq1, k5, sq1, k4.
Beg p row, work in St st for 3 rows.
9th row: K4, sq1, k5, sq1, k7.
Beg p row, work in St st for 3 rows, so ending with 12th row p.
5th–12th rows form patt. Repeat these 8 rows until the scarf measures 79 in. (200 cm).
K one row. Bind off knitwise.

TO MAKE UP
RS facing, fold so that edges meet to form a tube, then mattress stitch back seam, not pulling the stitches up too tightly.

Fringe
Cut 12¹/₂ in. (32 cm) lengths of yarn without sequins to make 10 tassels with 3 strands in each. With back seam facing, insert crochet hook through both layers at center of one end of scarf, catch 3 doubled strands, and pull them through to make a loop. Insert the hook in the loop, pull the strands through, and tighten. Make a tassel at each corner and then fill the spaces between with a tassel. Tassel opposite end in the same way. Using sewing needle, thread single sequins on random strands of fringe and knot the strands to hold the sequins in place.

Sequin knitting is slow but not difficult, and you'll create a classic that will shine at any party.

Sequin Tank Top

INTERMEDIATE

MEASUREMENTS

To fit bust

32	34	36	38	40	42	in.
81	86	91	97	102	107	cm

Actual bust

35	37	39	41	43	45	in.
89	94	99	104	109	114	cm

Actual length

19	$19^{1}/_{2}$	$20^{1}/_{4}$	21	$21^{1}/_{2}$	22	in.
48.5	50	51.5	53.5	54.5	56	cm

In the instructions, figures are given for the smallest size first; larger sizes follow in brackets. Where only one figure is given, this applies to all sizes.

MATERIALS

- 6 (2:2:2:3:3) × 100 g (3.53 oz) balls of Lion Brand Microspun in Mocha 124
- 8 (9:10:11:12:13) strands of 1,000 flat $^{1}/_{2}$ in. (10 mm) sequins, FS10, shade 9
- Pair of US 3 ($3^{1}/_{4}$ mm) needles

GAUGE

24 sts and 34 rows to 4 in (10 cm) over sequin patt on US (3) $3^{1}/_{4}$ mm needles. Change needle size if necessary to obtain this gauge.

ABBREVIATIONS

pfb—purl into front and back of st; **sq1**—bring a sequin up close to back of work and k next st through back of loop, drawing sequin through to RS as st is formed; **[ ]**—work instructions in brackets as directed.
See also page 10.

NOTES

- Thread sequins onto the yarn before starting to knit.
- Although the sequins are flat, they do have a very slight curve. Thread the sequins with the upper side of the curve toward the ball of yarn. If your sequins are not on strands, check that they face the same way before threading them.

BACK

Cast on 95 (101:107:113:119:125) sts.
1st row: (RS) K1, [sq1, k1] to end.
2nd and 4th rows: P.
3rd row: K2, [sq1, k1] to last st, k1.
These 4 rows form the sequin patt.
Cont in patt, work 33 more rows, so ending with a 1st patt row.
Inc row: (WS) Pfb, p to last 2 sts, pfb, p1.
Cont in patt, inc in this way at each end of every 8th row 5 times. [107 (113:119:125:131:137) sts.]

■ *Sequins for knitting should always be bought on strands, because this makes it easier to thread them onto the yarn.*

■ *Thread one strand of sequins at a time. When you run out of sequins, cut the yarn at the start of a row and thread on another strand of sequins. Never join a new strand in the middle of a row.*

■ *Sequin knits should be hand-washed.*

■ *Never iron sequins, they will curl or melt.*

Patt 25 (27:29:31:33:35) rows, so ending with a RS row.

Shape armholes
Bind off 5 sts at beg of next 2 rows. P 1 row.
Dec row: (RS) K2tog, patt to last 2 sts, skp.
Cont in patt, dec in this way at each end of next 8 (9:10:11:12:13) RS rows.
[79 (83:87:91:95:99) sts **.]
Patt 37 (37:39:41:41:43) rows.

Shape neck
Next row: (RS) Patt 17 (18:19:20:21:22), turn and complete right side on these sts. P 1 row.
Dec row: (RS) Patt to last 2 sts, skp.
Cont in patt, dec in this way at end of next RS row. [15 (16:17:18:19:20) sts.]
P 1 row. Bind off.
With RS facing, leave center 45 (47:49:51:53:55) sts on a holder, patt to end. [17 (18:19:20:21:22) sts.]
P 1 row.
Dec row: (RS) K2tog, patt to end.
Cont in patt, dec in this way at beg of next RS row. [15 (16:17:18:19:20) sts.]
P 1 row. Bind off.

FRONT
Beg 3rd patt row, work as given for back to **.
Patt 9 (9:11:13:13:15) rows.

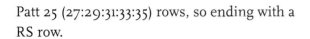

Shape neck
Next row: (RS) Patt 28 (29:30:31:32:33), turn and complete left side on these sts. P 1 row.
Dec row: (RS) Patt to last 2 sts, skp.
Cont in patt, dec in this way at end of next 12 RS rows. [15 (16:17:18:19:20) sts.]
Patt 7 rows. Bind off.
With RS facing, leave center 23 (25:27:29:31:33) sts on a holder, patt to end.
[28 (29:30:31:32:33) sts.] P 1 row.
Dec row: (RS) K2tog, patt to end.
Cont in patt, dec in this way at beg of next 12 RS rows. [15 (16:17:18:19:20) sts.]
Patt 7 rows. Bind off.

TO MAKE UP
Join left shoulder.
Neck edging: Pick up and k 5 sts down right back neck, patt across 45 (47:49:51:53:55) sts from holder, pick up and k 4 sts up left back neck and 24 sts down left front neck, patt across 23 (25:27:29:31:33) sts from holder, pick up and k 25 sts up right front neck. [126 (130:134:138:142:146) sts.] P 1 row.
Next row: (RS) K2, [sq1, k1] to end. Bind off knitwise.
Armhole edgings: Pick up and k 92 (96:102:108:112:118) sts around left armhole edge. Complete as given for neck edging. Join right shoulder seam and work right armhole edging to match. Join side seams.

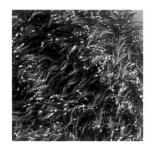

This super-soft, brushed yarn is shot through with random bursts of metallic gold, giving a sophisticated effect to the simplest of knitted coverups.

Glitter Wrap

 EASY

MEASUREMENTS

Actual width
24³/₄ in.
63 cm

Actual length
62 in.
158 cm

MATERIALS

- 13 × 50 g (1.76 oz) balls of Karabella Piuma Gold in Burgundy 10
- Pair of US 8 (5 mm) knitting needles
- 39¹/₂ in. (100 cm) long circular US 8 (5 mm) needle

GAUGE

20 sts and 26 rows to 4 in. (10 cm) over St st on US 8 (5 mm) needles. Change needle size if necessary to obtain this gauge.

ABBREVIATIONS

[ ]—work instructions in brackets as directed.
See also page 10.

NOTES

- Checking your gauge isn't easy when you can't see the stitches! Before measuring, hold your sample up to the light to count and mark the stitches, then turn it over to bump your thumbnail down the ridges to count and mark the rows.
- If you want to measure the length of the center of the wrap rather than count the rows, just remember to lie your knitting flat and spread out the stitches to the full width before measuring the length. Karabella makes a floppy, flexible fabric that will stretch when held up.
- If you find that the metallic gold patches clump together, use two balls of yarn, working 2 rows alternately with each to break up the patches.
- To pick up stitches evenly, divide the long edges into 6 sections and pick up 50 stitches from each section and one extra stitch from the center. Divide the short ends into two sections. and pick up 54 stitches from each section and one extra stitch from the center.
- If you want a simpler knit, just work the center without the frilled edge. You'll need only 7 balls of yarn and your wrap will measure 21¹/₂ in. (55 cm) wide and 59 in. (150 cm) long.

CENTER

Cast on 110 sts.
Beg k row, work in St st for 390 rows.
Bind off loosely.

EDGING

With RS facing and using circular needle,
pick up and k 301 sts along one long edge.
1st row: K.
2nd row: (RS) P3, [k1, p1] to last 4 sts, k1, p3.
3rd row: K3, [yo, p1, yo, k5] to last 4 sts, yo, p1,
yo, k3.
4th row: P3, [k3, p5] to last 6 sts, k3, p3.
5th row: K3, [yo, p3, yo, k5] to last 6 sts, yo, p3,
yo, k3.
6th row: P3, [k5, p5] to last 8 sts, k5, p3.
7th row: K3, [yo, p5, yo, k5] to last 8 sts, yo, p5,
yo, k3.
8th row: P3, [k7, p5] to last 10 sts, k7, p3.
Bind off loosely in rib.
Work 2nd long edging in the same way.
Pick up and k 109 sts along one short edge.
Work as given for first long edge.
Work 2nd short edging in the same way.

TO MAKE UP

Darn in ends. Join corner seams.

Cover up glamorously in a chunky cardigan with dense zigzag ribs and fully fashioned shapings.

One-Button Cardigan

ADVANCED

MEASUREMENTS

To fit bust

32–34	36–38	in.
81–86	91–97	cm

Actual bust

34¹/₂	39¹/₄	in.
88	100	cm

Actual length

18¹/₂	19³/₄	in.
47	50	cm

Actual sleeve length

17³/₄	17³/₄	in.
45	45	cm

In the instructions, figures are given for the smaller size first; the larger size follows in brackets. Where only one figure is given, this applies to both sizes.

MATERIALS

- 28 (30) × 25 g (0.88 oz) balls of Rowan Lurex Shimmer in Pewter, 333
- Pair of US 7 (4¹/₂ mm) knitting needles

GAUGE

30 sts and 28 rows to 4 in. (10 cm) over patt on US 7 (4¹/₂ mm) needles with yarn used double.

ABBREVIATIONS

d inc—double increase: k in back then front of st, insert lefthand needle point behind the vertical strand that runs downward from between the 2 sts just made and k in back of this strand, so making 3 sts from one; **m1p**—make a st by picking up strand in front of next st and p in back of it; **t2k**—twist 2 sts knitwise on RS rows: take needle behind first st on left hand needle and k in back of 2nd st, k in front of first st, then slip both sts off tog; **t2p**—twist 2 sts purlwise on WS rows: take needle in front of first st on lefthand needle and p 2nd st, p first st, then slip both sts off tog. *See also page 10. For illustrations of t2k and t2p, seep page 18.*

NOTES

- Yarn is used double throughout.
- Increases and decreases are alternately single and double in order to keep the stitch pattern correct.

BACK

Cast on 154 (178) sts.
1st row: (RS) P2, * t2k, p2; rep from * to end.
2nd row: K2, * t2p, k2; rep from * to end.
Rep 1st and 2nd rows 6 times more.
15th row: (RS) P2tog, * t2k, p2tog; rep from * to end. ** [115 (133) sts.] Now patt as follows:
1st row: (WS) K1, * t2p, k1; rep from * to end.
2nd row: P1, * t2k, p1; rep from * to end.

These 2 rows form patt. Rep 1st and 2nd patt rows 5 (7) times more, then 1st patt row again. *** 1st inc row: (RS) P1, t2k, d inc, patt to last 4 sts, d inc, t2k, p1.
Next row: K1, t2p twice, patt to last 5 sts, t2p twice, k1. Patt 6 rows as set.
2nd inc row: (RS) P1, t2k, m1p, patt to last 3 sts, m1p, t2k, p1. Patt 7 rows. ***
Rep from *** to *** twice more. [133 (151) sts.]

Shape armholes

Bind off 6 (9) sts at beg of next 2 rows.
1st dec row: (RS) P1, t2k, p3tog, patt to last 6 sts, p3tog, t2k, p1.
Next row: K1, t2p, k2, patt to last 5 sts, k2, t2p, k1.
2nd dec row: P1, t2k, p2tog, patt to last 5 sts, p2tog, t2k, p1.
Next row: Patt to end. ****
Rep these 4 rows 3 (4) times more.
[97 (103) sts.] Patt 28 rows straight.

Shape neck

1st row: (RS) Patt 22 (25), p3tog, t2k, p1, turn. Cont on these sts only for first side and leave rem sts on a spare needle.
Cont to dec at neck edge as for armhole shaping on next 5 RS rows. [19 (22) sts.]
Patt one row, so ending with a WS row.
Bind off firmly.
Next row: (RS) Rejoin yarn to inner end of rem sts, firmly bind off center 41 sts, t2k, p3tog, patt to end.
Complete to match first side.

RIGHT FRONT

Cast on 86 (98) sts.
Work as beg of back to **. [64 (73) sts.]
Patt 13 (17) rows straight. ***

Shape front and side

1st row: (RS) Patt 6, p3tog, patt to last 4 sts, d inc, t2k, p1. Patt 3 rows as set.
5th row: Patt 6, p2tog, patt to end. Patt 3 rows.
9th row: Patt 6, p3tog, patt to last 3 sts, m1p, t2k, p1. Cont to dec at front edge on every foll 4th row, working alternately p2tog and p3tog, while at the same time inc at side edge on every foll 8th row, working alternate double and single incs, until a total of 6 inc rows has been completed.
Cont to shape front edge as before, patt 8 rows straight at side edge, so ending with a RS row. [53 (62) sts.]

Shape armhole

Bind off 6 (9) sts at beg of next row.
Next row: (RS) Patt to last 6 sts, p3tog, t2k, p1.
Cont to shape front edge as before, at the same time cont to dec as back armhole until 8 (10) dec rows have been completed.
Keeping armhole edge straight, cont to dec at front edge as before until 25 (28) sts rem.
Patt straight until front matches back to shoulder, so ending with a WS row.

Neckband extension

Next row: Patt 7 sts, turn. Cont on these sts

■ *To prevent the yarn from tangling, keep a rubber band around each ball and release a short length of yarn as you work.*

only and leave rem 18 (21) sts on a st holder. Patt straight until extension, slightly stretched, fits to center back neck. Bind off firmly.

Shape shoulder

Next row: (RS) Rejoin yarn to inner end of rem 18 (21) sts, bind off firmly.

LEFT FRONT

As right front to ***.

Shape side and front

1st row: (RS) P1, t2k, d inc, patt to last 9 sts, p3tog, patt 6.
Cont to match right front, reversing armhole shaping by working one row less to armhole. Cont until front matches back to shoulder, so ending with a WS row.

Neckband extension

Next row: Bind off 18 (21) sts, patt across rem 7 sts. Complete as right neckband extension.

SLEEVES

Cast on 61 (64) sts.
1st row: (RS) P1, * t2k, p1, rep from * to end.
2nd row: K1, *t2p, k1; rep from * to end.
Rep these 2 rows 3 (7) times more.
1st inc row: (RS) P1, t2k, d inc, patt to last 4 sts, d inc, t2k, p1. Patt 7 (5) rows as set.
2nd inc row: P1, t2k, m1p, patt to last 3 sts, m1p, t2k, p1.
Cont to inc in this way, alternating double and

single inc rows, on every foll 8th (6th) row until a total of 14 (16) inc rows has been completed. [103 (112) sts.]
Patt straight until work measures $17^3/4$ in. (45 cm), ending with a WS row.

Shape top

Work as back armhole shaping to ****.
Rep last 4 rows 8 (9) times more. [37 (34) sts.]
Bind off 3 sts at beg of next 4 rows.
Firmly bind off rem 25 (22) sts.

TO MAKE UP

Join shoulder seams. Join ends of neckband extensions and sew inner edge around back neck. Set in sleeves. Join side and sleeve seams.

Slip on a small waistcoat that's a richly patterned brocade of interwoven cables in fine metallic yarn.

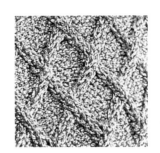

Cabled Vest

INTERMEDIATE

MEASUREMENTS

To fit bust

32–34	36–38	40–42	in.
81–86	91–97	102–107	cm

Actual measurement across back

17³/4	19³/4	21¹/2	in.
45	50	55	cm

Actual length

15	17	19¹/4	in.
38	43.5	49	cm

In the instructions, figures are given for the smallest size first; larger sizes follow in brackets. Where only one figure is given, this applies to all sizes.

MATERIALS

- 10 (11:12) × 25 g (0.88 oz) balls of Rowan Lurex Shimmer in Antique White Gold, 332
- Pair each of US 1 (2¹/4 mm) and US 3 (3 mm) knitting needles
- US 1 (2¹/4 mm) circular needle, 39¹/2 in. (100 cm) long
- Cable needle

GAUGE

48 sts and 43 rows to 4 in. (10 cm) over patt on US 3 (3 mm) needles.

ABBREVIATIONS

c4b—sl next 2 sts onto cable needle and hold at back, k2 then k2 from cable needle; **c4f**—as c4b but hold cable needle at front; **c4bp**—sl next 2 sts onto cable needle and hold at back, k2 then p2 from cable needle; **c4fp**—sl next 2 sts onto cable needle and hold at front, p2 then k2 from cable needle; **[ ]**—work instructions in brackets as directed. *See also page 10.*

BACK

Using US 1 (2¹/4 mm) needles, cast on 148 (164:180) sts. K 4 rows.
Inc row: (RS) K3, inc 1, * k4, [inc 1] 4 times; rep from * to last 8 sts, k4, inc 1, k3. **
[218 (242:266) sts.]
Change to US 3 (3 mm) needles and patt as follows or from chart on page 78:
1st row: (WS) K1, p2, k8, * p4, k8; rep from * to last 3 sts, p2, k1.
2nd row: P1, k2, * p8, c4b; rep from * to last 11 sts, p8, k2, p1.
3rd row: As 1st row.
4th row: P1, * c4fp, p4, c4bp; rep from * to last st, p1.
5th and WS rows: K all k sts and p all p sts as they appear.

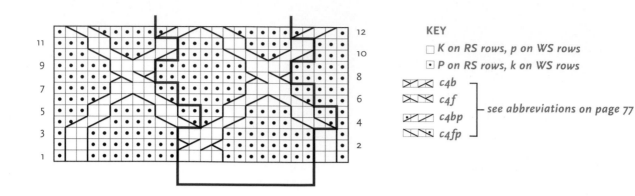

KEY
☐ K on RS rows, p on WS rows
• P on RS rows, k on WS rows
◿◺ c4b ⎤
◸◹ c4f ⎥ — see abbreviations on page 77
◿◸ c4bp ⎥
◺◹ c4fp ⎦

6th row: P3, * c4fp, c4bp, p4; rep from * to last 11 sts, c4fp, c4bp, p3.

8th row: P5, * c4f, p8; rep from * to last 9 sts, c4f, p5.

10th row: P3, * c4bp, c4fp, p4; rep from * to last 11 sts, c4bp, c4fp, p3.

12th row: P1, c4bp, * p4, c4fp, c4bp; rep from * to last 9 sts, p4, c4fp, p1.

Alternatively, work 1st–12th rows of chart, reading odd-numbered WS rows from left to right and even-numbered RS rows from right to left.

These 12 rows form patt. Rep 1st–12th rows 5 (6:7) times more, then work 1st–7th rows again, so ending with a WS row.

Shape armholes

Slipping the first st of each group of sts, bind off 3 sts at beg of next 24 (28:32) rows.
[146 (158:170) sts.]
Cont straight until 3rd row of 13th (15th:17th) patt has been completed, so ending with a WS row.

Shape neck

1st row: Patt across 44 (50:56) sts, turn. Cont on these sts only for first side and leave rem sts on a spare needle.
Dec one st at neck edge on next 6 rows.
[38 (44:50) sts.]
Patt 5 rows straight, so ending with a WS row.
Bind off, working each pair of p sts as p2tog.

Next row: (RS) Rejoin yarn to inner end of rem sts, bind off center 58 sts, working each pair of p sts as p2tog, then patt to end.
Complete to match first side.

LEFT FRONT

Using US 1 (2¼ mm) needles, cast on 52 (60:68) sts.
Work as beg of back to **. [74 (86:98) sts.]
Change to US 3 (3 mm) needles. ***
Patt as back until 7th row of 7th (8th:9th) patt has been completed.

Shape armhole

Slipping first st of each group of sts, bind off 3 sts at beg of next 12 (14:16) RS rows.
[38 (44:50) sts.]
Patt straight until work matches back to shoulder, so ending with a WS row.
Bind off, working each pair of p sts as p2tog.

RIGHT FRONT

Work as left front to ***.
Cont as back until 8th row of 7th (8th:9th) patt has been completed.

Shape armhole

Slipping the first st of each group of sts, bind off 3 sts at beg of next 12 (14:16) WS rows.
[38 (44:50) sts.]
Complete to match left front.

■ *Patterning on every RS row requires a certain amount of dexterity, so use a crook-style cable needle to reduce the risk of the double-pointed needle cable slipping out of the work.*

■ *The cable stitch pattern is given as row-by-row instructions and as a chart, so choose which method you prefer.*

FRONT BAND

Join shoulder seams.

With RS facing and using US 1 (2¹/₄ mm) circular needle, pick up and k 3 sts from right front edging, 120 (138:156) sts from edging to shoulder, 9 sts down right back neck, 40 sts across back neck, 9 sts up left back neck, 120 (138:156) sts down left front and 3 sts from left front edging. [304 (340: 376) sts.]

K 2 rows.

Bind off knitwise.

ARMHOLE EDGING

With RS facing and using US 1 (2¹/₄ mm) needles, pick up and k 3 sts from each group of 3 bind-off sts of right back armhole, then 40 (52:64) sts to shoulder seam, 40 (52:64) sts down right front armhole, and 3 sts from each group of 3 bind-off sts of right front armhole. [152 (188:224) sts.]

K one row.

Next row: (RS) [K4, k2tog] 6 (7:8) times, k to last 36 (42:48) sts, [k2tog, k4] 6 times. [140 (174:208) sts.]

Bind off knitwise.

Work left armhole edging to match.

TO MAKE UP

Iron lightly according to ball band.

Join side seams.

Shine softly in a close-fitting ribbed tube with a little lace-patterned bib front.

Lace Panel Top

 ADVANCED

MEASUREMENTS

To fit bust

32	34	36	38	in.
81	86	91	97	cm

Actual size, stretched

32	34	36	38	in.
81	86	91	97	cm

Actual length to underarm

8^1/$_2$	9	9^1/$_2$	10	in.
22	23	24	25	cm

In the instructions, figures are given for the smallest size first; larger sizes follow in brackets. Where only one figure is given, this applies to all sizes.

MATERIALS

- 5 (5:6:6) × 25 g (0.88 oz) balls Rowan Lurex Shimmer in Claret, 331
- Pair of US 1 (2^1/$_4$ mm) knitting needles
- 35^1/$_2$ in. (90 cm) narrow ribbon

GAUGE

33 sts and 42 rows to 4 in. (10 cm) over stretched rib on US 1 (2^1/$_4$ mm) needles.

ABBREVIATIONS

sk2p—sl one st knitwise, k 2 tog, pass slipped st over; **tbl**—through the back of the loop. *See also page 10.*

BACK

Cast on 113 (123:131:141) sts.
1st row: (RS) P1, * k1tbl, p1; rep from * to end.
2nd row: K1, * p1tbl, k1; rep from * to end.
These 2 rows form rib. Rep 1st and 2nd rows 4 times more.
11th row: (RS) P1, k1tbl, m1, rib to last 2 sts, m1, k1tbl, p1.
12th row: K1, p1tbl twice, rib to last 3 sts, p1tbl twice, k1.
13th row: P1, k1tbl twice, rib to last 3 sts, k1tbl twice, p1.
Rep 12th and 13th rows 5 times more, then work 12th row again.
25th row: As 11th row.
Keeping rib correct, inc one st at each end of every foll 14th row until 6 inc rows have been completed. [125 (135:143:153) sts.]
Rib 11 (15:19:23) rows straight, so ending with a WS row. **
Bind off loosely in rib.

FRONT

Work as back to **.
Lace panel Also refer to chart on page 83.)
Bind off 26 (26:30:30) sts at beg of next 2 rows. [73 (83:83:93) sts.]Now patt as follows:
1st row: (RS) P1, skp, rib to last 3 sts, k 2tog, p1.

■ *The lace stitch is explained in the row-by-row instructions as well as the chart. If you haven't used a chart before, you can refer from one to the other.*

2nd row: Beg and ending k1 and working each dec as p1tbl, rib to end.

3rd row: P1, skp, rib 10, [k2tog, yo, k1tbl, yo, skp, rib 5] 4 (5:5:6) times, k2tog, yo, k1tbl, yo, skp, rib 10, k2tog, p1.

4th row: Rib 12, [p1tbl, p1, p1tbl, p1, p1tbl, rib 5] 4 (5:5:6) times, p1tbl, [p1, p1tbl] twice, rib 12.

5th row: P1, skp, rib 8, [k2tog, yo, k3tbl, yo, skp, p1, k1tbl, p1] 4 (5:5:6) times, k2tog, yo, k3tbl, yo, skp, rib 8, k2tog, p1.

6th row: Work sts as presented, working each dec as p1tbl and each yo as p1.

7th row: P1, skp, rib 6, [k2tog, yo, k5tbl, yo, skp, k1tbl] 4 (5:5:6) times, k2tog, yo, k5tbl, yo, skp, rib 6, k2tog, p1.

8th row: As 6th row.

9th row: P1, skp, rib 4, k2tog, yo, k1tbl, [k2tog, yo 3 times, sk2p, k1tbl, yo, sk2p, yo, k1tbl] 4 (5:5:6) times, k2tog, yo 3 times, sk2p, k1tbl, yo, skp, rib 4, k2tog, p1.

10th row: As 6th row but working each triple yo as k1, p1, k1.

11th row: P1, skp, rib 5, [yo, skp, k3tbl, k2tog, yo, k3tbl] 4 (5:5:6) times, yo, skp, k3tbl, k2tog, yo, rib 5, k2tog, p1.

12th row: As 6th row.

13th row: P1, skp, rib 5, [yo, skp, k1tbl, k2tog, yo, k5tbl] 4 (5:5:6) times, yo, skp, k1tbl, k2tog, yo, rib 5, k2tog, p1.

14th row: As 6th row.

15th row: P1, skp, rib 5, [yo, sk2p, yo, k1tbl, k2tog, yo 3 times, sk2p, k1tbl] 4 (5:5:6) times, yo, sk2p, yo, rib 5, k2tog, p1.

16th row: As 10th row.

17th row: P1, skp, rib 2, [k2tog, yo, k3tbl, yo, skp, k3tbl] 4 (5:5:6) times, k2tog, yo, k3tbl, yo, skp, rib 2, k2tog, p1.

18th row: As 6th row.

19th row: P1, skp, [k2tog, yo, k5tbl, yo, skp, k1tbl] 4 (5:5:6) times, k2tog, yo, k5tbl, yo, skp, k2tog, p1. [53 (63:63:73) sts.]

Now patt without side shaping:

20th row: (WS) K1, p1tbl to last st, k1.

21st row: P1, k2tog, yo, k1tbl, [k2tog, yo 3 times, sk2p, k1tbl, yo, sk2p, yo, k1tbl] 4 (5:5:6) times, k2tog, yo 3 times, sk2p, k1tbl, yo, skp, p1.

22nd row: As 20th row and working k1, p1, k1 into each triple yo.

23rd row: P1, k2tbl, [yo, skp, k3tbl, k2tog, yo, k3tbl] 4 (5:5:6) times, yo, skp, k3tbl, k2tog, yo, k2tbl, p1.

24th row: As 20th row.

25th row: P1, k3tbl, [yo, skp, k1tbl, k2tog, yo, k5tbl] 4 (5:5:6) times, yo, skp, k1tbl, k2tog, yo, k3tbl, p1.

26th row: As 20th row.

27th row: P1, k4tbl, [yo, sk2p, yo, k1tbl, k2tog, yo 3 times, sk2p, k1tbl] 4 (5:5:6) times, yo, sk2p, yo, k4tbl, p1.

28th row: As 22nd row.

29th row: P1, k2tbl, [k2tog, yo, k3tbl, yo, skp, k3tbl] 4 (5:5:6) times, k2tog, yo, k3tbl, yo, skp, k2tbl, p1.

30th row: As 20th row.

31st row: P1, k1tbl, [k2tog, yo, k5tbl, yo, skp,

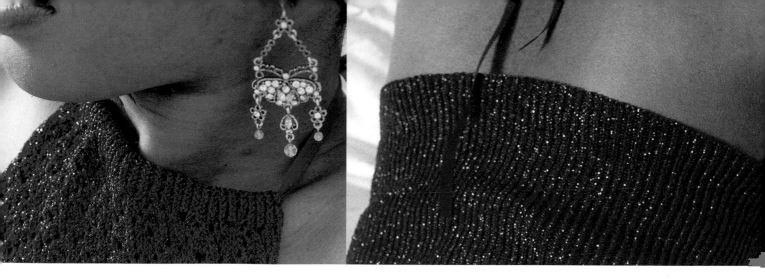

k1tbl] 5 (6:6:7) times, p1.

20th–31st rows form lace patt. Rep 20th–31st rows 2 (2:2:3) times more, then patt 3 (9:9:3) more rows.

Next row: (RS) P1, *k1tbl, p1; rep from * to end. Cont to rib as set for 10 rows. Bind off in rib.

TO MAKE UP

Join side seams. Turn rib at top of lace panel in half to the wrong side and catch down. Thread ribbon through this casing.

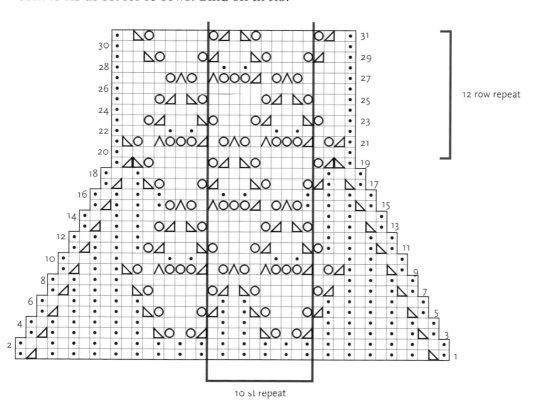

12 row repeat

10 st repeat

Key

☐   K1tbl on RS rows, p1 tbl on WS rows *

▪   P1 on RS rows, k1 on WS rows

O   Yo

◿   K2tog

◺   Skp

△   sk2p

Note

* Odd-numbered RS rows are read from right to left.

* Even-numbered WS rows are read from left to right.

* The exception to p1 tbl on WS rows is where a yo has been worked on the previous row. A single yo is worked p1 on the WS row, and a triple yo is worked k1, p1, k1.

Get a touch of country and western glamor with this shaped and fitted, studded and spangled, denim knit.

Studded Denim Jacket

INTERMEDIATE

MEASUREMENTS

To fit bust

32	34	36	38	40	42	44	in.
81	86	91	97	102	107	112	cm

Actual bust

33^1/$_4$	35^1/$_2$	37^1/$_2$	39^1/$_2$	41^3/$_4$	45^1/$_4$	46	in.
84.5	90	95	100.5	106	115.5	117	cm

Actual length (after washing)

19	19^1/$_4$	20	20^3/$_4$	21^1/$_4$	22	22^1/$_2$	in.
48	49	51	53	54	56	57	cm

Actual sleeve length (after washing)

17^3/$_4$	17^3/$_4$	18	18	18	18^1/$_2$	18^1/$_2$	in.
45	45	46	46	46	47	47	cm

In the instructions, figures are given for the smallest size first; larger sizes follow in brackets. Where only one figure is given, this applies to all sizes.

MATERIALS

- 10 (9:10:11:12:13:14) × 50 g (1.76 oz) balls of Rowan Denim in Memphis 229
- Pair each of US 3 (3^1/$_4$ mm) and US 6 (4 mm) needles
- 9 buttons
- 200 white metal round, domed studs
- Assorted clear glass stones, sequins, and silvery beads
- Metallic silver sewing thread and sharp needle

GAUGE

22 sts and 30 rows to 4 in. (10 cm) over St st, before washing, on US 6 (4 mm) needles. Change needle size if necessary to obtain gauge.

ABBREVIATIONS

sd st—seed stitch; **pfb**—purl into front and back of st; [ ]—work instructions in brackets as directed. *See also page 10.*

NOTE

- Rowan Denim in Memphis 229 is designed to fade and shrinks by 5% in length after the first wash. The instructions allow for this.

BACK

Using US 3 (3^1/$_4$ mm) needles, cast on 83 (89:95:101:107:113:119) sts.
1st row: (RS) P1, [k1, p1] to end.
This row forms sd st. Sd st 7 more rows.
Change to US 6 (4 mm) needles.
1st row: (RS) Sd st 5, k13 (15:17:19:21:23:25), sd st 5, k37 (39:41:43:45:47:49), sd st 5, k13 (15:17:19:21:23:25), sd st 5.
2nd row: Sd st 5, p13 (15:17:19:21:23:25), sd st 5, p37 (39:41:43:45:47:49), sd st 5, p13 (15:17:19: 21:23:25), sd st 5.
These 2 rows form St st at center and sides

■ *You can play around with the spacing of the studs by pushing them into the knitted fabric. The prongs will hold them in place, but they can easily be repositioned. When you're happy with the effect, use jewelers' chain-nosed pliers, tweezers, or the end of a metal nail file to bend the prongs over the yarn on the wrong side of the knitted fabric.*

■ *The sequins on the yoke are square, but round sequins would work just as well.*

■ *If your jeans have brass buttons, decorate your jacket with studs, stones, and sequins in yellow metal shades of copper, brass, and gold tones.*

■ *For a smoother line, slip the first stitch of each bind-off group when shaping the sleeve top.*

with 5 sts in sd st between panels and at vent edges. Work 8 more rows.

Vent tops

1st row: (RS) Sd st 3, k15 (17:19:21:23:25:27), sd st 5, k37 (39:41:43:45:47:49), sd st 5, k15 (17: 19:21:23:25:27), sd st 3.

2nd row: P1, k1, p16 (18:20:22:24:26:28), sd st 5, p37 (39:41:43:45:47:49), sd st 5, p16 (18:20: 22:24:26:28), k1, p1.

3rd row: P1, k17 (19:21:23:25:27:29), sd st 5, k37 (39:41:43:45:47:49), sd st 5, k17 (19:21:23: 25:27:29), p1.

4th row: Pfb, p17 (19:21:23:25:27:29), sd st 5, p37 (39:41:43:45:47:49), sd st 5, p17 (19:21:23: 25:27:29), pfb. [85 (91:97:103:109:115:121) sts.]

Next row: K19 (21:23:25:27:29:31), sd st 5, k37 (39:41:43:45:47:49), sd st 5, k19 (21:23:25: 27:29:31).

Cont in St st with 5 sts in sd st between panels, work 5 rows.

1st dec row: (RS) K2, k2tog, k12 (14:16:18:20: 22:24), skp, k1, sd st 5, k37 (39:41:43:45: 47:49), sd st 5, k1, k2tog, k12 (14:16:18:20: 22:24), skp, k2. [81 (87:93:99:105:111:117) sts.]
Work 5 rows.

2nd dec row: (RS) K2, k2tog, k10 (12:14:16:18: 20:22), skp, k1, sd st 5, k37 (39:41:43:45: 47:49), sd st 5, k1, k2tog, k10 (12:14:16:18: 20:22), skp, k2. [77 (83:89:95:101:107:113) sts.]
Work 11 rows.

1st inc row: (RS) K1, inc 1, k11 (13:15:17:19:21:23), inc 1, k1, sd st 5, k37 (39:41:43:45:47:49), sd st 5, inc 1, k11 (13:15:17:19:21:23), inc 1, k2. [81 (87:93:99:105:111:117) sts.]
Work 7 rows.

2nd inc row: (RS) K1, inc 1, k13 (15:17:19:21: 23:25), inc 1, k1, sd st 5, k37 (39:41:43:45:47:49), sd st 5, inc 1, k13 (15:17:19:21:23:25), inc 1, k2. [85 (91:97:103:109:115:121) sts.]
Work 7 rows.

3rd inc row: (RS) K1, inc 1, k15 (17:19:21:23: 25:27), inc 1, k1, sd st 5, k37 (39:41:43:45:47:49), sd st 5, inc 1, k15 (17:19:21:23:25:27), inc 1, k2. [89 (95:101:107:113:119:125) sts.]
Work 7 rows.

4th inc row: (RS) K1, inc 1, k17 (19:21:23:25: 27:29), inc 1, k1, sd st 5, k37 (39:41:43:45:47:49), sd st 5, inc 1, k17 (19:21:23:25:27:29), inc 1, k2. [93 (99:105:111:117:123:129) sts.]
Work 27 (29:29:31:31:33:33) rows.

Shape armholes

Bind off 4 (5:5:6:6:7:7) sts at beg of next 2 rows.

Dec row: K3, k2tog, patt to last 5 sts, skp, k3.
Dec in this way at each end of next 3 (4:5:6: 7:8:9) RS rows. [77 (79:83:85:89:91:95) sts.]
Work 17 (17:19:21:23:25:25) rows.

Yoke

Change to US 3 (3¼ mm) needles. Beg k1 (k1:p1:p1:k1:k1:p1), sd st 5 rows.
Change to US 6 (4 mm) needles. Beg p row, work in St st for 25 (25:27:27:27:27:27) rows.

Shape shoulders

Bind off 8 (9:9:10:10:11:11) sts at beg of next
2 rows and 9 (9:10:10:11:11:12) sts at beg of foll
2 rows. [43 (43:45:45:47:47:49) sts.]
Bind off.

LEFT FRONT

Using US 3 (3¹/₄ mm) needles, cast on 44
(47:50:53:56:59:62) sts. Ending RS rows and
beg WS rows, k1 for 1st, 3rd, 5th, and 7th sizes,
sd st 8 rows as given for back. Change to US 6
(4 mm) needles.
1st row: (RS) Sd st 5, k13 (15:17:19:21:23:25),
sd st 5, k16 (17:18:19:20:21:22), sd st 5.
2nd row: Sd st 5, p16 (17:18:19:20:21:22),
sd st 5, p13 (15:17:19:21:23:25), sd st 5.
These 2 rows form St st at center and side with
5 sts in sd st at vent edging, between panels, and
at front edge for band. Work 8 more rows.

Vent top

1st row: (RS) Sd st 3, k15 (17:19:21:23:25:27),
sd st 5, k16 (17:18:19:20:21:22), sd st 5.
2nd row: Sd st 5, p16 (17:18:19:20:21:22),
sd st 5, p16 (18:20:22:24:26:28), k1, p1.
3rd row: P1, k17 (19:21:23:25:27:29), sd st 5, k16
(17:18:19:20:21:22), sd st 5.
4th row: Sd st 5, p16 (17:18:19:20:21:22),
sd st 5, p17 (19:21:23:25:27:29), pfb. [45 (48:51:
54:57:60:63) sts.]
Next row: K19 (21:23:25:27:29:31), sd st 5,
k16 (17:18:19:20:21:22), sd st 5.
Cont in St st with 5 sts in sd st between panels

and at front edge, work 5 rows.
1st dec row: (RS) K2, k2tog, k12 (14:16:18:20:
22:24), skp, k1, sd st 5, k16 (17:18:19:20:
21:22), sd st 5. [43 (46:49:52:55:58:61) sts.]
Work 5 rows.
2nd dec row: (RS) K2, k2tog, k10 (12:14:16:18:
20:22), skp, k1, sd st 5, k16 (17:18:19:20:
21:22), sd st 5. [41 (44:47:50:53:56:59) sts.]
Work 11 rows.
1st inc row: (RS) K1, inc 1, k11 (13:15:17:19:21:23),
inc 1, k1, sd st 5, k16 (17:18:19:20:21:22), sd st 5.
[43 (46:49:52:55:58:61) sts.]
Work 7 rows.
2nd inc row: (RS) K1, inc 1, k13 (15:17:19:21:
23:25), inc 1, k1, sd st 5, k16 (17:18:19:20:21:22),
sd st 5. [45 (48:51:54:57:60:63) sts.]
Work 7 rows.
3rd inc row: (RS) K1, inc 1, k15 (17:19:21:23:
25:27), inc 1, k1, sd st 5, k16 (17:18:19:20:21:22),
sd st 5. [47 (50:53:56:59:62:65) sts.]
Work 7 rows.
4th inc row: (RS) K1, inc 1, k17 (19:21:23:25:
27:29), inc 1, k1, sd st 5, k16 (17:18:19:20:21:22),
sd st 5. [49 (52:55:58:61:64:67) sts.]
Work 27 (29:29:31:31:33:33) rows.

Shape armhole

Bind off 4 (5:5:6:6:7:7) sts at beg of next row.
Patt 1 row.
Dec row: (RS) K3, k2tog, patt to end.
Dec in this way at beg of next 3 (4:5:6:7:8:9)
RS rows. [41 (42:44:45:47:48:50) sts.]
Work 17 (17:19:21:23:25:25) rows.

Yoke

Change to US 3 (3¹/₄ mm) needles. Beg k1
(k1:p1:p1:k1:k1:p1), sd st 5 rows.
Change to US 6 (4 mm) needles.
Next row: (WS) Sd st 5, p to end.
Next row: K to last 5 sts, sd st 5.
Cont in St st with sd st 5 for band, work
7 rows.

Shape neck

1st row: (RS) K31 (32:33:34:35:36:37), turn
and leave 10 (10:11:11:12:12:13) sts on a holder
for neck.
2nd row: Slipping first st, bind off 2 sts,
p to end.
3rd row: K to last 2 sts, skp.
Work 2nd and 3rd rows 3 more times, then
work 2nd row again.
[17 (18:19:20:21:22:23) sts.]
St st 6 (6:8:8:8:8:8) rows, so ending with a
p row.

Shape shoulder

Bind off 8 (9:9:10:10:11:11) sts at beg of next row
and 9 (9:10:10:11:11:12) sts at beg of foll RS row.
Place markers for 8 buttons on WS rows, the
top one in line with the band of seed stitch
across the yoke, the lowest about 3¹/₂ in (9 cm)
from lower edge, with 6 more spaced evenly
between. The 9th buttonhole will be in the
collar.

RIGHT FRONT

Using US 3 (3¹/₄ mm) needles, cast on 44
(47:50:53:56:59:62) sts.
Beg RS rows and ending WS rows k1 for 1st,
3rd, 5th, and 7th sizes, sd st 8 rows as given
for back. Change to US 6 (4 mm) needles.
1st row: (RS) Sd st 5, k16 (17:18:19:20:21:22),
sd st 5, k13 (15:17:19:21:23:25), sd st 5.
2nd row: Sd st 5, p13 (15:17:19:21:23:25), sd st 5,
p16 (17:18:19:20:21:22), sd st 5.
These 2 rows form St st at center and side
with 5 sts in sd st at vent edging, between
panels, and at front edge for band. Work 8
more rows.

Vent top

1st row: (RS) Sd st 5, k16 (17:18:19:20:21:22),
sd st 5, k15 (17:19:21:23:25:27), sd st 3.
2nd row: P1, k1, p16 (18:20:22:24:26:28),
sd st 5, p16 (17:18:19:20:21:22), sd st 5.
3rd row: Sd st 5, k16 (17:18:19:20:21:22),
sd st 5, k17 (19:21:23:25:27:29), p1.
4th row: Pfb, p17 (19:21:23:25:27:29), sd st 5,
p16 (17:18:19:20:21:22), sd st 5. [45 (48:51:54:
57:60:63) sts.]
Next row: Sd st 5, k16 (17:18:19:20:21:22),
sd st 5, k19 (21:23:25:27:29:31).
Cont in St st with 5 sts in sd st between panels
and at front edge, work 5 rows.
Cont as given making buttonholes opposite
markers.
Buttonhole row: (WS) Patt to last 5 sts, p1, k1,
yo, skp, p1.

1st dec row: (RS) Sd st 5, k16 (17:18:19:20: 21:22), sd st 5, k1, k2tog, k12 (14:16:18: 22:24), skp, k2. [43 (46:49:52:55:58:61) sts.] Work 5 rows.

2nd dec row: (RS) Sd st 5, k16 (17:18:19:20: 21:22), sd st 5, k1, k2tog, k10 (12:14:16:18: 20:22), skp, k2. [41 (44:47:50:53:56:59) sts.] Work 11 rows.

1st inc row: (RS) Sd st 5, k16 (17:18:19:20: 21:22), sd st 5, inc 1, k11 (13:15:17:19:21:23), inc 1, k2. [43 (46:49:52:55:58:61) sts.] Work 7 rows.

2nd inc row: (RS) Sd st 5, k16 (17:18:19:20: 21:22), sd st 5, inc 1, k13 (15:17:19:21:23:25), inc 1, k2. [45 (48:51:54:57:60:63) sts.] Work 7 rows.

3rd inc row: (RS) Sd st 5, k16 (17:18:19:20: 21:22), sd st 5, inc 1, k15 (17:19:21:23:25:27), inc 1, k2. [47 (50:53:56:59:62:65) sts.] Work 7 rows.

4th inc row: (RS) Sd st 5, k16 (17:18:19:20: 21:22), sd st 5, inc 1, k17 (19:21:23:25:27:29), inc 1, k2. [49 (52:55:58:61:64:67) sts.] Work 28 (30:30:32:32:34:34) rows.

Shape armhole
Bind off 4 (5:5:6:6:7:7) sts at beg of next row.
Dec row: (RS) Patt to last 5 sts, skp, k3.
Dec in this way at end of next 3 (4:5:6:7:8:9) RS rows. [41 (42:44:45:47:48:50) sts.]
Work 17 (17:19:21:23:25:25) rows.

Yoke
Change to US 3 (3¼ mm) needles. Sd st 5 rows. Change to US 6 (4 mm) needles.
Next row: (WS) P to last 5 sts, sd st 5.
Next row: Sd st 5, k to end.
Cont in St st with sd st 5 for band, work 7 rows.

Shape neck
1st row: (RS) Sd st 5, k5 (5:6:6:7:7:8) and leave these 10 (10:11:11:12:12:13) sts on a holder for neck, k to end. [31 (32:33:34:35:36:37) sts.]
2nd row: P to last 2 sts, p2tog.
3rd row: Slipping first st, bind off 2 sts, k to end.
Work 2nd and 3rd rows 3 more times, then work 2nd row again.
Next row: (RS) K2tog, k to end. [17 (18:19:20: 21:22:23) sts.]
St st 6 (6:8:8:8:8:8) rows, so ending with a k row.

Shape shoulder
Bind off 8 (9:9:10:10:11:11) sts at beg of next row and 9 (9:10:10:11:11:12) sts at beg of foll WS row.

SLEEVES
Using US 3 (3¼ mm) needles, cast on 47 (49:49:51:53:53:55) sts. Sd st 8 rows as back. Change to US 6 (4 mm) needles. Beg k row, work in St st for 10 rows.
Inc row: (RS) K1, inc 1, k to last 3 sts, inc 1, k2.
Cont in St st, inc in this way at each end of every 10th (10th:10th:8th:8th:6th:6th) rows 8 (9:11:13:14:16:17 times. [65 (69:73:79:83:87:91) sts.]

Work in St st until sleeve measures 18³/₄ (18³/₄:19:19:19: 19¹/₂:19¹/₂) in. (47.5 (47.5:48.5:48.5:48.5:49.5:49.5 cm) ending with a p row.

Shape top

Bind off 4 (5:5:6:6:7:7) sts at beg of next 2 rows.
Dec row: K1, k2tog, patt to last 3 sts, skp, k1.
Dec in this way at each end of next 3 (4:5:6: 7:8:9) RS rows. [49 (49:51:53:55:55:57) sts.]
Work in St st for 5 (5:7:7:7:9:9) rows. Dec as before at each end of next 8 RS rows. [33 (33:35:37:39:39:41) sts.] P 1 row.
Bind off 2 sts at beg of next 4 rows and 4 sts at beg of foll 2 rows. [17 (17:19:21:23:23:25) sts.]
Bind off.

COLLAR

Join shoulders. Using US 3 (3¹/₄ mm) needles, slip 10 (10:11:11:12:12:13) sts from right front holder, pick up and k 23 (23:25:25:25:25:25) sts up right front neck, 43 (43:45:45:47:47:49) sts across back neck and 23 (23:25:25:25:25:25) sts down left front neck, k5 (5:6:6:7:7:8), sd st 5 from holder. [109 (109:117:117:121:121:125) sts.]
1st row: (RS) [P1, k1] to last 3 sts, yo, skp, p1.
2nd row: P1, [k1, p1] to end. This row forms sd st.
3rd row: Bind off 4 sts knitwise, sd st to end.
4th row: Bind off 4 sts purlwise, sd st to end. [101 (101:109:109:113:113:117) sts.] Cont in sd st until collar measures 4 in. (10 cm), ending with a RS row. Bind off loosely in sd st.

TO MAKE UP

Easing to fit, set in sleeves. Overlap front bands, and tack to secure in place. Wash and dry jacket. Take out tacking stitches. Set studs in rows spaced evenly along sd st between panels, across each side of yoke at the lower edge of the sleeves, and around the collar. Scatter remaining studs at random over yoke. Using metallic yarn, sew on glass stones between studs, then fill in the spaces between studs and stones with sequins. To hold each sequin in place, bring the needle up at the center hole, thread on a small bead, take the needle back through the hole, and secure on the wrong side. Join side seams to top of vents and sleeve seams. Sew on buttons.

Add lots of pearly beads and sequins to a simple cardigan and create an enduring classic.

Beaded Cardigan

★★☆

INTERMEDIATE

MEASUREMENTS

To fit bust

32	34	36	38	40	42	in.
81	86	91	97	102	107	cm

Actual bust

$33^1/_2$	$35^1/_2$	$37^3/_4$	$39^3/_4$	$41^1/_2$	44	in.
85	90	96	101	107	112	cm

Actual length

$19^3/_4$	$20^1/_2$	$20^3/_4$	$21^1/_2$	$22^1/_2$	$22^3/_4$	in.
50	52	53	55	57	58	cm

Actual sleeve length

$17^3/_4$	$17^3/_4$	$17^3/_4$	$17^3/_4$	$17^3/_4$	$17^3/_4$	in.
45	45	45	45	45	45	cm

In the instructions, figures are given for the smallest size first; larger sizes follow in brackets. Where only one figure is given, this applies to all sizes.

MATERIALS

- 8 (8:9:9:10:10) × 50 g (1.76 oz) balls RYC Cashsoft DK in Cream, 00500
- Pair of US 3 (3 mm), US 3 (3¹/₄ mm), US 5 (3³/₄ mm) and US 6 (4 mm) knitting needles
- Beads and sequins—10 large beads, a quantity of medium and small pearl beads, cup sequins, and bugle beads
- Fine sewing needles and sewing thread to match the knitting yarn
- Hooks and eyes

GAUGE

22 sts and 29 rows to 4 in. (10 cm) over St st on US 6 (4 mm) needles.

ABBREVIATIONS

[ ]—work instructions in brackets the number of times stated. *See also page 10.*

BACK

Using US 3 (3¹/₄ mm needles), cast on 90 (96:102:108:114:120) sts.
Beg k row, work in St st for 4 rows.
P next row to mark hemline.
Change to US 5 (3³/₄ mm) needles and beg p row, work in St st for 5 rows. **
Change to US 6 (4 mm) needles.
Dec row: (RS) K1, skp, k to last 3 sts, k2tog, k1.
Cont to dec in this way at each end of every foll 6th row until a total of 4 dec rows has been completed. [82 (88:94:100:106:112) sts.]
Beg p row, work in St st for 9 rows.
Inc row: (RS) K2, m1, k to last 2 sts, m1, k2.
Cont to inc in this way at each end of every foll 10th row until a total of 6 inc rows has been completed. [94 (100:106:112:118:124) sts.]
Beg and ending p row, work in St st for 7 (9:11:13:15:17) rows straight.

Shape armholes

Bind off 5 (5:5:6:6:6) sts at beg of next 2 rows, then dec as for beg of back at each end of next 8 (9:10:10:11:12) RS rows. [68 (72:76:80:84: 88) sts.] Beg p row, work in St st for 25 (27:27:29:31:31) rows straight.

Shape neck

1st row: (RS) K21 (23:24:26:27:29), k2tog, k1, turn.
Cont on these sts only for first side and leave rem sts on a spare needle.
2nd row: P.
3rd row: K to last 3 sts, k2tog, k1.
Rep 2nd and 3rd rows 4 times more.
P one row.
Leave rem 18 (20:21:23:24:26) sts on a spare needle.
Next row: (RS) Sl center 20 (20:22:22:24:24) sts onto a spare needle, rejoin yarn to inner end of rem sts, k1, skp, k to end.
Complete to match first side.

LEFT FRONT

Using US 3 (3¼ mm) needles, cast on 43 (46:49:52:55:58) sts.
1st row: K to last 2 sts, inc 1, k1.
2nd row: P.
Rep 1st and 2nd rows once. [45 (48:51:54:57: 60) sts.]
P next row to mark hemline.
Change to US 5 (3¾ mm) needles and beg p row, work in St st for 5 rows.

Change to US 6 (4 mm) needles.
Dec row: (RS) K1, skp, k to end.
Cont to dec in this way at beg of every foll 6th row until a total of 4 dec rows has been completed. [41 (44:47:50:53:56) sts.]
Beg p row, work in St st for 9 rows.
Inc row: (RS) K2, m1, k to end.
Cont to inc in this way at beg of every foll 10th row until a total of 6 inc rows has been completed. [47 (50:53:56:59:62) sts.]
Beg and ending p row, work in St st for 7 (9:11:13:15:17) rows straight.

Shape armhole

Bind off 5 (5:5:6:6:6) sts at beg of next row.
P one row.
Next row: (RS) K1, skp, k to end.
Cont to dec in this way at beg of next 7 (8:9:9: 10:11) RS rows.
[34 (36:38:40:42:44) sts.]
Beg and ending p row, work in St st for 17 (19:19:21:23:23) rows straight.

Shape neck

1st row: (RS) K21 (23:24:26:27:29), k2tog, k1, turn.
Cont on these sts only and leave rem 10 (10:11: 11:12:12) sts on a st holder.
Dec as for first side of back neck on next 5 RS rows. [18 (20:21:23:24:26) sts.]
Beg and ending p row, work in St st for 9 rows straight.
Leave sts on a spare needle.

■ *Don't worry if you can't find beads and sequins exactly like those pictured—almost any mix of pearl and pale gold colors will work with this soft cream yarn.*

RIGHT FRONT

Using US 3 (3¹/₄ mm) needles, cast on
43 (46:49:52:55:58) sts.

1st row: Inc 1, k to end.

2nd row: P.

Rep 1st and 2nd rows once. [45 (48:51:54:57:
60) sts.]

P next row to mark hemline.

Change to US 5 (3³/₄ mm) needles and beg p
row, work in St st for 5 rows.

Change to US 6 (4 mm) needles.

Dec row: (RS) K to last 3 sts, k2tog, k1.

Cont to match left front, working one more
row to armhole shaping and working each
armhole dec as k2tog. [34 (36:38:40:42:44) sts.]

Beg and ending p row, work in St st for 17
(19:19:21:23:23) rows straight.

Shape neck

1st row: (RS) Break yarn, sl first 10 (10:11:11:
12:12) sts onto a st holder, rejoin yarn at inner
edge of rem sts, k1, skp, k to end.

Complete to match left front.

SLEEVES

Using US 3 (3¹/₄ mm) needles, cast on 46
(48:50:52:54:56) sts.

Work as beg of back to **.

Change to US 6 (4 mm) needles.

Beg k row, work in St st for 10 (6:0:10:4:0) rows.

Next row: (RS) K2, m1, k to last 2 sts, m1, k2.

Cont to inc in this way on every foll 10th
(10th:10th:8th:8th:8th) row until a total of

11 (12:13:14:15:16) inc rows has been completed.
[68 (72:76:80:84:88) sts.]

Work in St st straight until work measures
17³/₄ in. (45 cm) from hem line, ending p row.

Shape top

Bind off 5 (5:5:6:6:6) sts at beg of next 2 rows,
dec as for back armhole at each end of next 8
(9:10:10:11:12) RS rows. [42 (44:46:48:50:52) sts.]

Dec as before at each end of next 3 (3:3:4:4:4)
alternate RS rows. [36 (38:40:40:42:44) sts.]

Dec as before at each end of next 3 RS rows.
[30 (32:34:34:36:38) sts.]

Bind off 2 sts at beg of next 4 rows.

Bind off purlwise rem 22 (24:26:26:28:30) sts.

NECK FACING

Join shoulder seams by binding off tog sts of
front and back shoulders: with RS tog and using
US 6 (4 mm) needles, k tog one st from front
shoulder, one st from back shoulder each time.

With RS facing and using US 3 (3¹/₄ mm)
needles, k10 (10:11:11:12:12) sts from right front
neck, pick up and k18 sts to shoulder and 12 sts
down right back neck, k20 (20:22:22:24:24) sts
from back neck, pick up and k 12 sts up left back
neck and 18 sts down left front neck, k10
(10:11:11:12:12) sts from left front neck.
[100 (100:104:104:112:112) sts.]

K 2 rows.

3rd row: P2tog tbl, p to last 2 sts, p2tog.

4th row: K9 (9:10:10:11:11), m1, [k3, m1]
10 times, k20 (20:22:22:24:24), m1, [k3, m1]

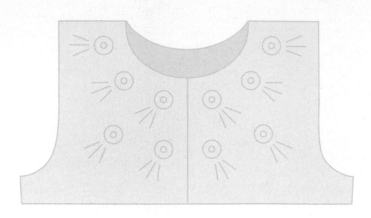

10 times, k9 (9:10:10:11:11).
5th row: As 3rd row.
Bind off.

FRONT FACINGS

With RS facing and using US 3 (3¹/₄ mm) needles, pick up and k96 (100:104:108:112:116) sts from hemline to neck facing on right front.
K2 rows.
3rd row: P2tog tbl, p to last 2 sts, p2tog.
4th row: K.
5th row: As 3rd row.
Bind off.
Work left front facing to match.

TO BEAD AND MAKE UP

Iron according to instructions on ball band. Turn hems and facings to wrong side, iron and catch down, joining mitered corners at neck and lower fronts.

Using stitches and rows as a guide, sew medium-sized pearl beads along all edges (see page 19 for how to sew on beads).

With contrast yarn, count rows and stitches to tack a grid of squares to act as a guide on the part of the fronts to be beaded. Arrange the centers of 5 "flowers" on one front, placing a large pearl bead in the center and 8 smaller ones around (see right). Stitch these in place, then use the grid to make the same arrangement on the opposite front and stitch this in place. Each time arranging and stitching a component on one front before matching it on the other, make a ring of cup sequins close together around each flower center and hold them in place with a tiny bead (see page 20). Sequins look livelier if the tones and colors are mixed and any translucent ones are used in pairs, one on top of another. Now scatter bugle beads near the flowers and cup sequins in the resulting spaces, becoming fewer around the back of the neck.

Set in sleeves. Join side and sleeve seams and hems with mattress stitch (see page 21) worked on the RS. Iron seams.

Finally, sew pairs of hooks and eyes to the front facings, a little way in from the edge.

Walk tall in this lean edge-to-edge fingertip-length coat that's knitted in a soft lightweight yarn with a subtle gleam.

Cigarette Coat

★☆☆ EASY

MEASUREMENTS

To fit bust

32–34	36–38	40–42	in.
81–86	91–97	102–107	cm

Actual bust

36	39^1/$_2$	43	in.
91.5	100.5	109	cm

Actual length

29^1/$_2$	30^1/$_4$	31^1/$_4$	in.
75	77	79.5	cm

Actual sleeve length

17^3/$_4$	17^3/$_4$	17^3/$_4$	in.
45	45	45	cm

In the instructions, figures are given for the smallest size first; larger sizes follow in brackets. Where only one figure is given, this applies to all sizes.

MATERIALS

- 10 (11:12) × 50 g (1.76 oz) balls of RYC Soft Lux in Powder, 002
- Pair of US 7 (4^1/$_2$ mm) knitting needles

GAUGE

18 sts and 32 rows to 4 in. (10 cm) over sd st on US 7 (4^1/$_2$ mm) needles.

ABBREVIATIONS

d inc—k in front, back, and front of st to make 3 sts from one; **sd st**—seed stitch.
See also page 10.

BACK

Cast on 95 (103:111) sts.
1st row: (RS) K1, * p1, k1; rep from * to end. This row forms sd st. Rep first row 19 times more.
21st row: (RS) K2tog, sd st to last 2 sts, skp. Keeping sd st correct, dec in this way at each end of every foll 20th row until a total of 6 dec rows has been completed. [83 (91:99) sts.]
Sd st straight until work is 21^1/$_2$ (22:22^1/$_2$) in (55 (56:57) cm) ending with a WS row.

Shape armholes

Bind off 3 (4:5) sts at beg of next 2 rows, then dec 1 st at each end of next 7 (8:9) RS rows. [63 (67:71) sts.]
Sd st 39 (41:43) rows straight, so ending with a WS row.

Shape neck

1st row: Sd st 21 (23:23) sts, turn. Cont on these sts only for first side and leave rem sts on a spare needle.
2nd row: Sd st.

When joining new yarn on the front sections, do this at the sides, and not the front, edges so that the ends can be darned into a seam.

3rd row: Sd st to last 6 sts, p3tog, k1, p1, k1.
Cont to dec in this way on next 2 RS rows.
[15 (17:17) sts.]
Sd st 3 rows.
Bind off in sd st.
Next row: (RS) Rejoin yarn to inner end of rem sts, bind off center 21 (21:25) sts, sd st to end. [21 (23:23) sts.]
Sd st one row.
Next row: (RS) K1, p1, k1, p3tog, sd st to end.
Cont to dec in this way on next 2 RS rows.
[15 (17:17) sts.]
Sd st 3 rows.
Bind off in sd st.

LEFT FRONT

Cast on 43 (47:51) sts.
Sd st 2 rows. **
3rd row: (RS) Sd st to last 3 sts, d inc, p1, k1.
Sd st 3 rows.
7th row: As 3rd row. [47 (51:55) sts.]
Sd st 13 rows.
21st row: K2tog, sd st to end.
Cont to dec in this way at beg of every foll 20th row until a total of 6 dec rows has been completed. [41 (45:49) sts.]
Sd st straight until work matches back to armhole shaping, so ending with a WS row.

Shape armhole
Bind off 3 (4:5) sts at beg of next row.
Dec one st at beg of next 7 (8:9) RS rows.
[31 (33:35) sts.]
Sd st 19 (21:23) rows straight, so ending with a WS row.

Shape neck
1st dec row: Sd st to last 6 sts, p3tog, k1, p1, k1.
Sd st 2 rows.
Next row: (WS) Bind off in sd st 8 (8:10) sts, sd st to end.
2nd dec row: As 1st dec row. Cont to dec in this way at end of next 2 RS rows.
[15 (17:17) sts.]
Sd st 21 rows straight.
Bind off in sd st.

RIGHT FRONT

As left front to **.
3rd row: (RS) K1, p1, d inc, sd st to end.
Sd st 3 rows.
7th row: As 3rd row. [47(51:55) sts.]
Sd st 13 rows straight.
21st row: (RS) Sd st to last 2 sts, skp.
Cont to match left front, working one more row to armhole, so ending with a RS row.

Shape armhole
Bind off 3 (4:5) sts at beg of next row, then dec one st at end of next 7 (8:9) RS rows. [31 (33:35) sts.]
Sd st 19 (21:23) rows straight, so ending with a WS row.

Shape neck

1st dec row: K1, p1, k1, p3tog, sd st to end.
Sd st one row.
Next row: (RS) Bind off 8 (8:10) sts,
sd st to end.
Sd st one row.
2nd dec row: As 1st dec row.
Cont to dec in this way at beg of next 2 RS
rows. [15 (17:17) sts.]
Sd st 21 rows straight.
Bind off in sd st.

SLEEVES

Cast on 43 (45:47) sts.
Sd st 16 (6:6) rows.
Next row: (RS) K1, m1, sd st to last st, m1, k1.
Keeping sd st correct, cont to inc in this way at
each end of every foll 16th (16th:14th) row until
a total of 8 (9:10) inc rows has been
completed. [59 (63:67) sts.]
Sd st straight until work measures 17³/₄ in
(45 cm) ending with a WS row.

Top shaping

Bind off 3 (4:5) sts at beg of next 2 rows.
Next row: (RS) K2tog, sd st to last 2 sts, skp.
Cont to dec in this way on next 6 (7:8) RS
rows. [39 sts.]
Dec in this way at each end of every 4th row
2 times.
Dec in this way at each end of next 7 RS rows.
Bind off rem 17 sts in sd st.

TO MAKE UP

Carefully pinning out rounded corners on
fronts, iron according to instructions on ball
band. Join shoulder seams. Set in sleeves. Join
side and sleeve seams.

BLACK AND WHITE

Get that graphic look in dramatic black or laser-bright white. Luxuriate in the texture of a quick-to-knit, fun fur bolero, or create a film star effect with a super-furry hat and long, lacy mittens. Knit the sweater equivalent of the ever useful little black dress with optional slits and slashes, go for a demure beaded lacy sweater, dare to bare your back in a laced-up corset top, or get a quick style-fix with a '60s look sequin and loop-knit bag.

Enjoy cuddling into the luscious thick pile of this little furry bolero.

Furry Bolero

 EASY

MEASUREMENTS

To fit bust

32	34	36	38	40	42	in.
81	86	91	97	102	107	cm

Actual measurement across back

16	$17^1/_4$	$18^1/_2$	$19^3/_4$	$21^1/_4$	$22^1/_2$	in.
41	44	47	50	54	57	cm

Actual length

11	$12^1/_2$	13	$13^3/_4$	15	$15^3/_4$	in.
28	31	33	35	38	40	cm

Actual sleeve length

8	8	$8^1/_4$	$8^1/_4$	$8^1/_2$	$8^1/_2$	in.
20	20	21	21	22	22	cm

In the instructions, figures are given for the smallest size first; larger sizes follow in brackets. Where only one figure is given, this applies to all sizes.

MATERIALS

- 4 (8:9:9:10:10) × 100 g (3.53 oz) balls of Crystal Palace Splash in Ivory
- Pair of US 10¹/₂ (7 mm) knitting needles

GAUGE

12³/₄ sts and 17 rows to 4 in. (10 cm) over St st on US 10¹/₂ (7 mm) needles.

ABBREVIATIONS

See page 10.

BACK

Cast on 45 (49:53:57:61:65) sts.
Beg k row, work in St st for 2 rows.
3rd row: (RS) Inc 1, k to last 2 sts, inc 1, k1.
Beg p row, cont in St st, inc one st as before at each end of every foll 4th row until a total of 4 inc rows has been completed. [53 (57:61:65:69:73) sts.]
Beg and ending p row, work in St st for 3 (5:7:9:11:13) rows straight.

Shape armholes
Bind off 3 (3:4:4:5:5) sts at beg of next 2 rows.
Next row: (RS) K1, k2tog, k to last 3 sts, skp, k1.
Cont to dec in this way at each end of next 3 (4:4:5:5:6) RS rows. [39 (41:43:45:47:49) sts.]
Beg and ending p row, work in St st for 17 (17:19:19:21:21) rows straight.

Shape neck
1st row: (RS) K11 (12:13:14:15:16) sts, turn.
Leave rem sts on a spare needle and cont on these sts only for first side.
2nd row: P1, p 2 tog through back of loops, p to end.
3rd row: K to last 3 sts, skp, k1.
Rep 2nd row, then bind off rem 8 (9:10:11:12:13) sts.

■ *Counting rows can be difficult when working with a textured yarn, so use markers—either readymade ones or lengths of contrast yarn slipped between stitches.*

■ *After making up, run the point of a needle along the seams to free any trapped pile and the seams will be completely invisible.*

Next row: (RS) Rejoin yarn to inner end of rem sts, bind off center 17 sts, k to end.
2nd row: P to last 3 sts, p 2 tog, p1.
3rd row: K1, k2tog, k to end.
Rep 2nd row, then bind off rem 8 (9:10:11: 12:13) sts.

LEFT FRONT
Cast on 12 (14:16:18:20:22) sts.
1st row: (RS) K to last 2 sts, inc 1, k1.
2nd and WS rows: P.
3rd row: Inc 1, k to last 2 sts, inc 1, k1.
5th row: K to last 2 sts, inc 1, k1.
** Cont to inc at front edge on every RS row and also at side edge on next and every 4th row until 15 rows have been completed. [24 (26:28:30:32:34] sts.] ***
Beg and ending p row, work in St st for 3 (5:7:9:11:13) rows straight.

Shape armhole
Bind off 3 (3:4:4:5:5) sts at beg of next row.
P one row.
Next row: (RS) K1, k2tog, k to end.
Cont to dec in this way at beg of next 3 (4:4:5:5:6) RS rows. [17 (18:19:20:21:22) sts.]
P one row.

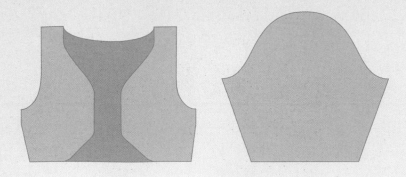

Shape front edge

1st row: (RS) K to last 3 sts, skp, k1.
Cont to dec in this way at end of next 8 RS
rows. [8 (9:10:11:12:13) sts.]
Beg and ending p row, work in St st for
3 (3:5:5:7:7) rows straight.
Bind off.

RIGHT FRONT

Cast on 12 (14:16:18:20:22) sts.
1st row: (RS) Inc 1, k to end.
2nd and WS rows: P.
3rd row: Inc 1, k to last 2 sts, inc 1, k1.
5th row: Inc 1, k to end.
Cont as given for left front from ** to ***.
Beg p row and ending k row, work in St st
for 4 (6:8:10:12:14) rows straight.

Shape armhole

Bind off 3 (3:4:4:5:5) sts at beg of next row.
Next row: (RS) K to last 3 sts, skp, k1.
Cont to dec in this way at end of next 3 (4:4:
5:5:6) RS rows. [17 (18:19:20:21:22) sts.]
P one row.

Shape front edge

1st row: (RS) K1, k2tog, k to end.
Cont to dec in this way at beg of next 8 RS
rows. [8 (9:10:11:12:13) sts.]
Beg and ending p row, work in St st for
3 (3:5:5:7:7) rows straight. Bind off.

SLEEVES

Cast on 32 (34:37:39:42:44) sts.
Beg k row, work in St st for 4 (4:6:6:8:8) rows.
Next row: (RS) Inc 1, k to last 2 sts, inc 1, k1.
Cont to inc in this way on every foll 6th row
until there are 42 (44:47:49:52:54) sts.
Beg and ending p row, work in St st for 5 rows
straight.

Shape top

Bind off 3 (3:4:4:5:5) sts at beg of next 2 rows.
Next row: (RS) K1, k2tog, k to last 3 sts,
skp, k1.
Cont to dec in this way at each end of next
3 (4:4:5:5:6) RS rows. [28 (28:29:29:30:30) sts.]
Dec 1 st at each end of every foll 4th row
3 times. [22 (22:23:23:24:24) sts.]
Dec 1 st at each end of next 3 rows as for back
neck shaping.
Bind off rem 16 (16:17:17:18:18) sts.

TO MAKE UP

Join shoulder seams. Set in sleeves. Join side
and sleeve seams.

Sling this '6os style bag over your shoulder for instant retro chic.

Sequin Shoulder Bag

EASY

MEASUREMENTS
9 in. (23 cm) wide × 6³/₄ in. (17 cm) deep

MATERIALS
- 4 × 100 g (3.53 oz) balls of Classic Elite Provence in Bleach 2601
- Pair each of US 3 (3¹/₄ mm) and US 5 (3³/₄ mm) knitting needles
- Oval paillette sequins
- Fine sewing needle and white sewing thread
- Two split rings

GAUGE
19 sts and 27 rows to 4 in. (10 cm) over patt on US 5 (3³/₄ mm) needles.

ABBREVIATIONS
lp1—make a loop: k the next st but do not slip it off the needle; bring the yarn to the front between the needles, take it under then over your left thumb and back between the needles; k the st on lefthand needle again and slip it off in the usual way, then pass the next st on the righthand needle over it. For an illustration see page 18. **g-st**—garter stitch: k every row. *See also page 10.*

BACK
Using US 5 (3³/₄ mm) needles, cast on 43 sts.

1st row: (RS) K1, * lp1, k1; rep from * to end.
2nd row: K1, p41, k1.
3rd row: K2, * lp1, k1; rep from * to last st, k1.
4th row: As 2nd row.
These 4 rows form pattern. Rep 1st—4th rows 9 times more, then work first row again, so ending with a RS row.
Change to US 3 (3¹/₄ mm) needles and g-st 4 rows. Bind off knitwise.

FRONT
As back.

HANDLE
Using US 3 (3¹/₄ mm) needles, cast on 205 sts. G-st 3 rows. Bind off knitwise.

TO MAKE UP
Placing front on back, wrong sides together, use the knitting yarn to back stitch side and base seams, one stitch in from edge. With sewing thread, randomly stitch paillettes to ends of loops, scattering them more thinly toward the top of the bag.
Insert a split ring through the front and back of the bag near each top corner. Use the knitting yarn to attach each end of the handle to a split ring, oversewing around the ring.

This sexy sweater is made from simple shaped strips of rolled edge stockinette stitch, with as big as you dare gaps left open when joining the seams.

Slits-and-Slashes Sweater

 EASY

MEASUREMENTS

Stretches to fit bust

32	34	36	38	40	42	in.
81	86	91	97	102	107	cm

Actual bust

$31^{1}/_{2}$	$33^{1}/_{2}$	36	38	$40^{1}/_{4}$	$42^{3}/_{4}$	in.
80	85.5	91	97	102.5	108.5	cm

Actual length

23	$23^{3}/_{4}$	$24^{1}/_{4}$	$24^{3}/_{4}$	$25^{1}/_{4}$	26	in.
58.5	60.5	61.5	63	64	66	cm

Actual sleeve length

18 in.
46 cm

In the instructions, figures are given for the smallest size first; larger sizes follow in brackets. Where only one set of figures is given, this applies to all sizes.

MATERIALS

- 6 (6:6:7:7:8) × 100 g (3.53 oz) balls of Lana Grossa Meilenweit in 1106 black
- Pair of US 3 ($3^{1}/_{4}$ mm) knitting needles

GAUGE

28 sts and 36 rows to 4 in. (10 cm) over St st on US 3 ($3^{1}/_{4}$ mm) needles. Change needle size if necessary to obtain this gauge.

ABBREVIATIONS

rev—reverse. [ ]—work instructions in square brackets as directed. *See also page 10.*

NOTES

- The back and front are each knitted in two halves, then joined leaving gaps.
- The sleeve is worked in the opposite way to the usual construction, so the inside arm increases normally made each side of the seam are in the center and the seam that will be joined with gaps runs up the outer arm.

RIGHT BACK

Cast on 62 (66:70:74:78:82) sts.
1st row: (RS) P3, k to last 3 sts, p3.
2nd row: K3, p to last 3 sts, k3.
These 2 rows form St st with 3 sts in rev St st at each side. Work 30 more rows **.
Dec row: (RS) P3, k2, k2tog, k to last 3 sts, p3.
Cont in St st with rev St st at each side, dec in this way at beg of every 6th row 5 times. [56 (60:64:68:72:76) sts.] Work 15 rows.
Inc row: (RS) P3, k1, inc 1, k to last 3 sts, p3.
Cont in St st with rev St st at each side, inc in this way at beg of every 6th row 5 times. [62 (66:70:74:78:82) sts.]
Work 33 (35:35:37:37:39) rows.

Shape armhole

Dec in same way as before at beg of next row and every RS row 10 (11:12:13:14:15) times. [51 (54:57:60:63:66) sts.]
Work 49 (51:53:55:57:59) rows. Bind off.

LEFT BACK

Work as given for right back to **.
Dec row: (RS) P3, k to last 7 sts, skp, k2, p3.
Cont in St st with rev St st at each side, dec in this way at end of every 6th row 5 times.
[56 (60:64:68:72:76) sts.]
Work 15 rows.
Inc row: (RS) P3, k to last 6 sts, inc 1, k2, p3.
Cont in St st with rev St st at each side, inc in this way at end of every 6th row 5 times. [62 (66:70:74:78:82) sts.]
Work 33 (35:35:37:37:39) rows.

Shape armhole

Dec in same way as before at end of next row and every RS row 10 (11:12:13:14:15) times. [51 (54:57:60:63:66) sts.]
Work 49 (51:53:55:57:59) rows. Bind off.

LEFT FRONT

Work as given for right back.

RIGHT FRONT

Work as given for left back.

SLEEVES

Cast on 60 (62:64:66:68:70) sts.
1st row: (RS) P3, k24 (25:26:27:28:29), p6,

■ *Mark each shaping with a loop of contrast smooth thread. Use the threads to help match the pieces when sewing up the sections.*

■ *You can join as much or as little of each of the seams as you wish.*

■ *Pin the back and front pieces together before sewing, and try on the sweater to make sure you are happy with the spacing of the gaps in the seams. Take the sweater off and check that the spacing is even before sewing.*

k24 (25:26:27:28:29), p3.

2nd row: K3, p24 (25:26:27:28:29), k6, p24 (25:26:27:28:29), k3.

These 2 rows form St st with 3 sts in rev St st at each side and 6 sts in rev St st at center.

Work 38 (30:30:22:22:14) more rows.

Inc row: (RS) P3, k until 3 sts before 6 sts at center, inc 1, k2, p6, k1, inc 1, k to last 3 sts, p3.

Cont inc in this way at each side of center 6 sts every 8th row 12 (13:14:15:16:17) times. [86 (90:94:98:102:106) sts.]

Work 29 (29:21:21:13:13) rows straight.

Shape top

1st row: (RS) P3, k33 (35:37:39:41:43), skp, k2, p3, turn and complete 1st side on these 42 (44:46:48:50:52) sts.

Noting that there will be one less k st before dec each time, dec in this way at end of next 10 (11:12:13:14:15) RS rows. [32 (33:34:35:36:37) sts.]

Work 7 rows straight.

Dec as before at end of next 21 (22:23:24:25:26) RS rows. [11 sts.]

Work 1 row. Bind off.

With RS facing, join yarn for 2nd side.

1st row: (RS) P3, k2, k2tog, k to last 3 sts, p3. [42 (44:46:48:50:52) sts.]

Dec in this way at beg of next 10 (11:12:13:14:15) RS rows. [32 (33:34:35:36:37) sts.] Work 7 rows straight.

Dec as before at beg of next 21 (22:23:24:25:26) RS rows. [11 sts.]

Work 1 row. Bind off.

TO MAKE UP

Iron all pieces according to ball band. Leaving six gaps open, mark position to join left and right back pieces along straight edges. With WS facing, using mattress stitch and omitting rolled edge sts to bring the RS of St st together, join approximately 6 rows at lower edge, between gaps and at top of center back seam. Marking positions for 4 gaps and leaving the top part of each piece free for collar, join center front seam in the same way. Join 19 (20:21:22:23:24) sts of back and front for each shoulder. Ending at start of armhole shaping, join side seams in the same way as the front. Join bind-off edges at sleeve top. Spacing gaps evenly, join straight edges of sleeves in the same way as back. Set in sleeves.

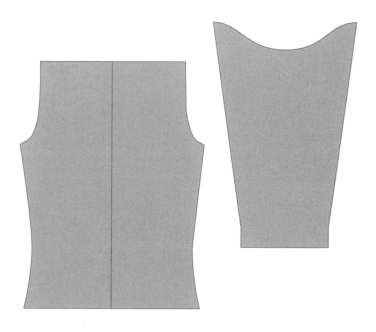

Ultra-long-faux fur yarn makes this simple hat look very dramatic. Wear it plain or add decoration for a special occasion.

Foxy Fur Hat

 EASY

MEASUREMENTS

Actual measurement around head
22 in.
56 cm

MATERIALS

- 3 × 50 g (1.76 oz) balls of Crystal Palace Splash in Ebony
- Pair of US 10½ (7 mm) needles

GAUGE

12½ sts and 17 rows to 4 in. (10 cm) over St st on US 10½ (7 mm) needles. Change needle size if necessary to obtain this gauge.

ABBREVIATIONS

sk2p—slip one knitwise, k2tog, pass slipped st over; [ ]—work instructions in brackets as directed. *See also page 10.*

NOTES

- If you'd rather knit to length for the brim, lay the work flat and make sure that it measures 8 in. (20 cm) wide before measuring the length. At the correct gauge the 77 rows will measure 17³/₄ in. (45 cm) but this will stretch to measure 22 in.(56 cm).
- When picking up the stitches for the crown, skip approximately every 11th row-end.

BRIM

Cast on 25 sts. Beg k row, work in St st for 77 rows. Bind off.

CROWN

With WS facing, pick up and k 71 sts along one long edge of the brim.
Beg p row, work in St st for 7 rows.

Shape top
1st dec row: (RS) K1, [k2tog, k5, skp, k1] 7 times. [57 sts.] P 1 row.
2nd dec row: K1, [k2tog, k3, skp, k1] 7 times. [43 sts.] P 1 row.
3rd dec row: K1, [k2tog, k1, skp, k1] 7 times. [29 sts.] P 1 row.
4th dec row: K1, [s2kpo, k1] 7 times. [15 sts.] P 1 row.
5th dec row: K1, [k2tog] 7 times. [8 sts.] Leaving a long end, cut yarn.

TO MAKE UP

Thread end through sts at top of crown, draw up, and secure. Join back seam, reversing seam for rolled up brim.

Dare to bare your back in this curvy little top with dramatic lace-up detail.

Corset Top

MEASUREMENTS

To fit bust

32	34	36	38	in.
81	86	91	97	cm

Actual front width at bust

15³/₄	16³/₄	17³/₄	19	in.
40	42.5	45	48	cm

Actual length

17³/₄	18	18¹/₂	19	in.
45	46	47	48	cm

In the instructions, figures are given for the smallest size first; larger sizes follow in brackets. Where only one figure is given, this applies to all sizes.

MATERIALS

- 4 (4:5:5) × 50 g (1.76 oz) balls of Debbie Bliss Cathay in black shade 01
- Pair of US 5 (3³/₄ mm) needles
- 39¹/₂ in. (100 cm) long US 5 (3³/₄ mm) circular needle
- 3¹/₄ yd (3 m) narrow black cord

GAUGE

22 sts and 30 rows to 4 in. (10 cm) over St st on US 5 (3³/₄ mm) needles. Change needle size if necessary to obtain this gauge.

ABBREVIATIONS

ssp—slip the first st knitwise, then the 2nd st, return sts to left needle, noting that they now face the opposite way to the other sts, take right needle behind and through 2nd, then first st to p2tog; [ ]—work instructions in brackets as directed. *See also page 10.*

NOTE

- Use straight needles or the circular needle to work the pieces of the top, but you will need to use the circular needle for the picot edging.

FRONT

Cast on 78 (84:90:96) sts. Beg k row, work in St st for 4 rows.

Dec row: (RS) K3, k2tog, k to last 5 sts, skp, k3. Cont in St st, dec in this way at each end of every 4th row 3 times. [70 (76:82:88) sts.] Work in St st for 5 rows.

Inc row: (RS) K2, inc 1, k to last 4 sts, inc 1, k3. Cont in St st, inc in this way at each end of every 6th row 9 times. [90 (96:102:108) sts.] Work in St st for 5 (5:7:7) rows.

Shape neck and armholes

1st row: (RS) K42 (45:48:51), skp, k1, turn and complete left side on these 44 (47:50:53) sts, leaving 45 (48:51:54) sts for right side.

■ Because the back laces up, it is not possible to give an actual bust measurement. If you are not sure which size to make, measure around your bust, divide the number in half, and make the nearest size. If in doubt, go for a slightly smaller rather than larger, size, because the knitting will stretch to fit.

■ If you are not familiar with working ssp, practice it on a sample swatch. It is easy to do, and you'll find that it gives the exact opposite of p2tog, so the stitches at the shaped edges of the front are mirror images.

2nd row: P1, ssp, p to end.
3rd row: Bind off 4 (5:5:6) sts, k to last 3 sts, skp, k1. [38 (40:43:45) sts.]
4th row: P1, ssp, p to end.
5th row: K1, k2tog, k to last 3 sts, skp, k1.
Work 4th and 5th rows 5 (6:7:8) more times. [20 (19:19:18) sts.] Dec as before at neck edge only on next 9 (7:6:4) rows. [11 (12:13:14) sts.] Work in St st for 30 (32:33:35) rows. Bind off. With RS facing, join yarn to remaining 45 (48:51:54) sts for right side.
1st row: (RS) K1, k2tog, k to end.
2nd row: P to last 3 sts, p2tog, p1.
3rd row: As 1st.
4th row: Bind off 4 (5:5:6) sts, p to last 3 sts, p2tog, p1. [37 (39:42:44) sts.]
5th row: K1, k2tog, k to last 3 sts skp, k1.
6th row: P to last 3 sts, p2tog, p1.
Work 5th and 6th rows 5 (6:7:8) more times. [19 (18:18:17) sts.]
Dec as before at neck edge only on next 8 (6:5:3) rows. [11 (12:13:14) sts.] Work in St st for 30 (32:33:35) rows. Bind off.

RIGHT BACK
Cast on 15 (18:20:23) sts. Beg k, St st 4 rows.
Dec row: (RS) K3, k2tog, k to end. Cont in St st, dec in this way at beg of every 4th row 3 times. [11 (14:16:19) sts.] Work in St st for 5 rows.
Inc row: (RS) K2, inc 1, k to end.
Cont in St st, inc in this way at beg of every 6th row 9 times. [21 (24:26:29) sts.]
Work in St st for 7 (7:9:9) rows.

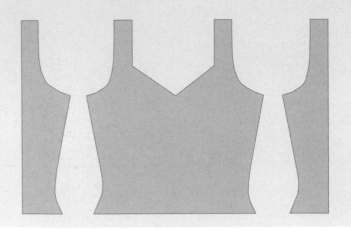

■ *When shaping the top of the sleeve, slip the first stitch of each bind-off group for a smoother line.*

■ *The cord is threaded through the picot points of the edging, so you can adjust the spacing and start higher up or lower down the back to get the fit that's best for you.*

Shape armhole

Bind off 4 (5:5:6) sts at beg of next row. P 1 row.
Dec row: (RS) K1, k2tog, k to end.
Cont in St st, dec in this way at beg of next 5 (6:7:8) RS rows. [11 (12:13:14) sts.] Work in St st for 39 rows. Bind off.

LEFT BACK

Cast on 15 (18:20:23) sts. Beg k, work in St st for 4 rows.
Dec row: (RS) K to last 5 sts, skp, k3.
Cont in St st, dec in this way at end of every 4th row 3 times. [11 (14:16:19) sts.] Work in St st for 5 rows.
Inc row: (RS) K to last 4 sts, inc 1, k3.
Cont in St st, inc in this way at end of every 6th row 9 times. [21 (24:26:29) sts.]
St st 8 (8:10:10) rows.

Shape armhole

Bind off 4 (5:5:6) sts at beg of next row.
Dec row: (RS) K to last 3 sts, skp, k1.
Cont in St st, dec in this way at end of next 5 (6:7:8) RS rows. [11 (12:13:14) sts.]
Work in St st for 39 rows. Bind off.

SLEEVES

Cast on 68 (72:74:78) sts. Beg k, work in St st for 2 rows.

Shape top

Bind off 4 (5:5:6) sts at beg of next 2 rows.
Dec row: (RS) K1, k2tog, k to last 3 sts, skp, k1.

Cont in St st, dec in this way at each end of next 13 (14:15:16) RS rows. [32 sts.] P 1 row.
[Bind off 2 sts at beg and work skp at end of next row. Bind off 2 sts at beg and work p2tog at end of foll row] 3 times. 14 sts. Bind off.

TO MAKE UP

Back and neck edging

Join shoulders. Using circular needle, pick up and k 97 (100:103:106) sts up left back. 18 (21:23:25) sts down left front neck to start of shaping, 24 (24:25:26) sts to center, one st from between center 2 sts, 24 (24:25:26) sts up right front neck shaping, 18 (21:23:25) sts to shoulder, and 97 (100:103:106) sts down right back. [279 (291:303:315) sts.] K 1 row.
Picot row: (RS) K2, bind off one st, [return st to left needle, cast on 2 sts, bind off 2 sts, k2tog, bind off one st, k1, bind off one st] to end, ending last repeat k1, bind off one st, fasten off.

Sleeve edgings

Pick up and k 69 (72:75:78) sts along cast-on edge. Complete as for back and neck edging.

Lower edging

Set in sleeves. Join side and sleeve seams. Pick up and k 13 (16:19:22) sts along lower right back edge, 76 (82:88:94) sts along front edge, and 13 (16:19:22) sts along left back edge. [102 (114:126:138) sts.] Complete as for back and neck edging. Thread lace through the holes in the picot edge at each side of the back. Adjust lacing.

This shapely pullover has a subtle lace pattern outlined with beads between the leafy panels.

Beaded Lacy Pullover

 ADVANCED

MEASUREMENTS

To fit bust

32	34	36	38	40	42	44	46	in.
81	86	91	97	102	107	112	117	cm

Actual bust

34¹/₂	36¹/₂	38	39³/₄	41¹/₂	43	45	46¹/₂	in.
88	92.5	97	101	105.5	109.5	114	118	cm

Actual length

22	22	23¹/₄	23¹/₄	25¹/₄	25¹/₄	26¹/₄	26¹/₄	in.
56	56	59	59	64	64	67	67	cm

Actual sleeve length

18	18	18	18	19	19	19	19	in.
45.5	45.5	45.5	45.5	48	48	48	48	cm

In the instructions, figures are given for the smallest size first; larger sizes follow in brackets. Where only one figure is given, this applies to all sizes.

MATERIALS

- 8 (4:4:5:5:5:6:6) × 100 g (3.53 oz) balls of Classic Elite Provence in Black 2613
- Pair of US 3 (3¹/₄ mm) needles
- 23¹/₂ in (60 cm) long US 3 (3¹/₄ mm) circular needle
- 17¹/₂ oz (500 g) (approximately 5,300) rocaille glass beads

GAUGE

28 sts to 4 in. (10 cm) over St st, 24 sts measure 3¹/₈ in. (8 cm), 30 rows to 4 in. (10 cm) over beaded lace patt on US 3 (3¹/₄ mm) needles. Change needle size if necessary to obtain these gauges.

ABBREVIATIONS

B—bring a bead up close to work; **sk2p**—slip one knitwise, k2tog, pass slipped st over; **ssk and pass**—slip the first st knitwise, then the 2nd, return sts to left needle, noting that they now face the opposite way and k2tog, slip st just made from right to left needle, lift 2nd st on left needle over first, return st to right needle; **[ ]**—work instructions in brackets as directed. *See also page 10.*

NOTES

- Work with beaded yarn throughout. Thread as many beads as is practical onto yarn before starting to knit. When there are not enough beads left to complete a row, cut yarn at the beginning of a row, thread on more beads and rejoin yarn. Never join in new yarn or add beads during a row.
- Cast on by the knitting-off-the-thumb method (see page 11)

■ The beads used for this design are metallic-coated glass beads. Although there will be some beads left over in the smaller sizes, a 17½ oz (500 g) pack (approximately 5,300 beads) is recommended for all sizes, because buying beads in smaller amounts can work out to be more expensive. This will also allow for some beads to be malformed or with holes too small to thread onto the yarn.

■ Because the beads hang between stitches, they do not need to be included in the stitch counts.

■ To keep the pattern correct on the smaller sizes, when decreasing for the armhole and top of the sleeve, it will be necessary to work k4tog at the beginning and slip one, k3tog, pass slipped stitch over at the end when the double decrease in the pattern reaches the edges.

■ Although metallic beads are used for the pullover in the photograph, you can use any beads you like as long as they have a hole that is large enough to thread them onto the yarn.

BACK

Sliding a bead up close between each st, cast on 126 (126:130:136:140:140:146:150) sts.

1st and every WS row: P2 (2:4:7:9:9:12:14), [k2, p10] to last 4 (4:6:9:11:11:14:16) sts, k2, p2 (2:4: 7:9:9:12:14).

2nd row: (RS) K2 (2:4:7:9:9:12:14), [p1, B, p1, k6, ssk and pass, yo, k1, yo, p1, B, p1, yo, k1, yo, sk2p, k6] to last 4 (4:6:9:11:11:14:16) sts, p1, B, p1, k2 (2:4:7:9:9:12:14).

4th row: K2 (2:4:7:9:9:12:14), * p1, B, p1, k4, ssk and pass, [k1, yo] twice, k1, p1, B, p1, [k1, yo] twice,

k1, sk2p, k4, rep from * to last 4 (4:6:9:11:11:14:16) sts, p1, B, p1, k2 (2:4:7:9:9:12:14).

6th row: K2 (2:4:7:9:9:12:14), [p1, B, p1, k2, ssk and pass, k2, yo, k1, yo, k2, p1, B, p1, k2, yo, k1, yo, k2, sk2p, k2] to last 4 (4:6:9:11:11: 14:16) sts, p1, B, p1, k2 (2:4:7:9:9:12:14).

8th row: K2 (2:4:7:9:9:12:14), [p1, B, p1, ssk and pass, k3, yo, k1, yo, k3, p1, B, p1, k3, yo, k1, yo, k3, sk2p] to last 4 (4:6:9:11:11:14:16) sts, p1, B, p1, k2 (2:4:7:9:9:12:14).

These 8 rows form the beaded lace patt.

Cont in patt, work 49 (49:41:41:41:25:25:17) more rows.

Inc row: (RS) Inc 1, patt to last 2 sts, inc 1, k1. Taking incs into St st at each side, cont in patt, inc in this way at each end of every 16th (8th:8th:8th:8th:8th:8th:8th) row 2 (5:6:6:7:10: 10:11) times.

[132 (138:144:150:156:162:168:174) sts.]

Patt 23 (15:15:15:15:7:7:7) rows.

Shape armholes

Bind off 3 (6:6:7:7:8:9:12) sts at beg of next 2 rows.

Keeping patt correct for smaller sizes, dec one st at each end of next 13 RS rows. [100 (100: 106:110:116:120:124:124) sts **.]

Taking sts at each side of patt into St st, patt 29 (29:37:37:45:45:53:53) rows. Bind off.

FRONT

Work as given for back to **.

Patt 20 (20:28:28:36:36:44:44) rows.

- *Although the cotton yarn can be machine washed, to protect the beads it's best to turn the pullover inside out and hand wash it. If you want to spin the pullover in a machine to remove excess water, put it in a washing bag or a pillowcase.*
- *If you want to make the pullover without the beads for a pretty, lacy, daytime knit, simply omit all the beads. Without the weight of the beads, the row gauge could be tighter, so be prepared to add more rows, if necessary, to get the desired length.*
- *Black is the classic winter party color. For a subtle effect you could use black glass instead of metallic beads. Other combinations of yarn and bead color could also work well, such as pastel and silver for a summer party or white and pearly beads for a wedding.*

Shape neck

Next row: (WS) P1(1:4:6:9:0:1:1) , k2 (2:2:2:2: 1:2:2), [p10, k2] 1 (1:1:1:1:2:2:2) times, p4, turn and complete right side on these 19 (19:22:24: 27:29:31:31) sts.

Dec row: (RS) K2tog, patt to end.

Cont in patt, dec in this way at beg of next 2 RS rows. [16 (16:19:21:24:26:28:28) sts.] Patt 3 rows. Bind off.

With WS facing, leave center 62 sts on a holder, patt to end. [19 (19:22:24:27:29:31:31) sts.]

Dec row: (RS) Patt to last 2 sts, skp.

Cont in patt, dec in this way at end of next 2 RS rows. [16 (16:19:21:24:26:28:28) sts.] Patt 3 rows. Bind off.

SLEEVES

Sliding a bead up close between each st, cast on 78 (78:82:88:92:92:98:102) sts. Work in patt as given for back for 81 (81:73:73:73:57: 57:49) rows. Inc in same way as back at each end of next row and on every 16th (8th:8th:8th:8th:8th:8th:8th) row 2 (5:6:6:7:10:10:11) times. [84 (90:96:102:108:114:120:126) sts] Patt 23 (15:15:15:15:7:7:7) rows.

Shape top

Bind off 3 (6:6:7:7:8:9:12) sts at beg of next 2 rows. Keeping patt correct, dec one st at each end of next row and on foll 14 (14:17:19:22: 24:26:26) RS rows. [48 sts.]

Patt 1 row. Bind off 2 sts at beg and dec one st at end of next 8 rows. [24 sts.] Bind off.

NECK EDGING

Matching sts, join shoulders. Using circular needle, pick up and k 68 sts across back neck and 8 sts down left front neck, patt across 62 sts from holder, pick up and k 8 sts up right front neck. [146 sts.] Sliding a bead up close between sts each time, bind off loosely purlwise.

TO MAKE UP

Laying pieces out with WS facing and using a pressing cloth to protect the beads, iron according to ball band to open the lace pattern. Set in sleeves. Join side and sleeve seams.

These pretty fingerless gloves are just simple, lacy tubes that are knitted in the round, so there are no seams and very little making up!

Lacy Fingerless Gloves

 INTERMEDIATE

MEASUREMENTS

Stretches to fit around hand
9¹/₂ in.
24 cm

Stretches to length
15 in.
38 cm

Actual measurement around glove
18 in.
20 cm

Actual length
10¹/₂ in.
27 cm

MATERIALS

- 50 g (1.76 oz) ball of Lana Grossa Meilenweit 50 in 1106 Black
- Set of US 3 (3¹/₄ mm) double pointed needles.
- 19¹/₂ in. (50 cm) of narrow black lacy lingerie elastic
- Black sewing thread and sharp needle

GAUGE

21 sts and 39 rows to 4 in. (10 cm) over lacy patt in the round, not stretched, on US 3 (3¹/₄ mm) needles. Change needle size if necessary to obtain this gauge.

ABBREVIATIONS

[ ]—work instructions in brackets as directed. *See also page 10.*

NOTE

- When joining to make a round, check that the stitches are not twisted on the needles.

FIRST GLOVE

Cast on 14 sts on each of 3 needles. [42 sts.]
Join in a round. K 1 round.
Next round: (WS) [Yo, p2tog] to end.
This round forms lacy patt. Work 105 more rounds. K 2 rounds.
Bind off round: K1, yo, bind off one st, [k1, bind off one st, yo, bind off one st] to end.
Fasten off.

SECOND GLOVE

Work as given for first mitt.

TO MAKE UP

Turn gloves inside out so right side faces. Try on, mark position, and stitch to make thumbholes in bind-off edges. Darn in ends. Sew lacy elastic around bind-off edges.

- *If you want longer gloves, weigh the remaining yarn while knitting the first glove and bind off when almost 1 oz (25 g) of yarn has been used. There should then be enough yarn to make the second glove the same length.*
- *The instructions are written for a set of 4 double-pointed needles. If you have a set of 5 needles, cast on 10 sts on each of the first 3 needles and 12 sts on the 4th needle, making a total of 42 sts.*
- *Why work with the wrong side facing? Because yarn over, p2tog is easier to work than yarn over, k2tog. Try it and see!*

Suppliers

Call for nearest distributor, or where available, order online.

USA

CLASSIC ELITE YARNS, INC.
122 Western Avenue
Lowell, MA 01851
Tel: (978) 453 2837
www.classiceliteyarns.com

CRYSTAL PALACE YARNS
160 23rd Street
Richmond, CA 94804
Tel: (510) 237 9988
www.crystalpalaceyarns.com

DMC CREATIVE WORLD
77 South Hackensack Avenue
Bldg. 10F
South Kearny, NJ 07032
Tel: (973) 589 0606
www.dmc-usa.com

LION BRAND YARN CO.
34 West 15th St.
New York, NY 10011
Tel: (212) 243-8995

For beads, sequins and trimmings:
M & J TRIMMING
1008 Sixth Avenue
New York, NY 10018
Tel: (800) 965 8746
www.mjtrim.com

MICHAELS STORES, INC.
8000 Bent Branch Drive
Irving, TX 75063
Tel: (800) 642 4235
www.michaels.com

For Debbie Bliss and Sirdar yarns:
KNITTING FEVER INC.
PO Box 336
315 Bayview Avenue
Amityville, NY 11701
Tel: (516) 546 3600
www.knittingfever.com

For Elle yarns:
UNICORN BOOKS AND CRAFTS INC.
1138 Ross Street
Petaluma, CA 94954
Tel: (707) 762 3362
Email: dcodling@unicornbooks.com

For Rowan, RYC and Jaeger yarns:
WESTMINSTER FIBERS INC.
4 Townsend West, Suite 8
Nashua, NH 03064
Tel: (603) 886 5041/5043
Email: rowan@westminsterfibers.com

CANADA

A. Bruneau Canada, Inc.
338 St-Antoine Street East,
Suite 011
Montreal, Quebec H2Y 1A3
Tel: (800) 361 8487

Lily Sugar & Cream Yarn
320 Livingstone Avenue South
Listowel, ON N4W 3H3
Tel: (888) 368 8401
www.sugarncream.com

UK

For Debbie Bliss yarns:
DESIGNER YARNS LTD
Units 8–10,
 Newbridge Industrial Estate
Pitt Street
Keighley
West Yorkshire, BD21 4PQ
Tel: (01535) 664222
Fax: (01535) 664333
www.designeryarns.uk.com

For Elle yarns:
QUADRA UK LTD
Tey Grove
Elm Lane
Feering
Essex, CO5 9ES
Tel: (01376) 573802
Email: quadrauk@aol.com

For Rowan, RYC and Jaeger yarns:
ROWAN
Green Lane Mill, Holmfirth
West Yorkshire, HD9 2DX
Tel: (01484) 681881
www.knitrowan.com

For Sirdar yarns:
SIRDAR SPINNING LTD
Flanshaw Lane, Alverthorpe,
Wakefield,
West Yorkshire, WF2 9ND
Tel: (01924) 371501
www.sirdar.co.uk

For beads, sequins and trimmings:
CREATIVE BEADCRAFT
Unit 2, Asheridge Business Centre
Asheridge Road, Chesham
Buckinghamshire, HP5 2PT
Tel: (01494) 778818
www.creativebeadcraft.co.uk

ELLS AND FARRIER
20 Beak Street
London, W1F 9RE
Tel: (020) 7629 9964
For personal shoppers only.

THE BEAD SHOP
21a Tower Street
London, WC2H 9NS
Tel: (020) 7240 0931

INDEX

ACKNOWLEDGEMENTS

Many thanks to Rosemary Wilkinson for giving us the opportunity to work together again. Thanks also to Clare Hubbard and everyone else involved in making this book.

  For the inspirational yarns, thanks to: Debbie Bliss and all at Designer Yarns; Mike Cole and all at Elle Yarns; Kate Buller and all at Rowan and Jaeger; David Rawson and all at Sirdar.

  For help with the knitting, thanks to: Brenda Bostock, Sally Buss, Helen Fraser, Gwen Radford, Jean Trehane and Hilary Underwood.

  Finally, but most important of all, thank you to Sue Horan for checking the instructions.